Exploring Branson

A Family Guide

W.C. Jameson

Library of Congress Cataloging-in-Publication Data

Jameson, W.C.
    Exploring Branson: a family guide   / by W.C. Jameson.
        p.   cm.
    Includes index.
    ISBN 1-55622-570-9 (pb.)
    1. Branson (Mo.)--Guidebooks.   I. Title.
    F474.B79J35   1998
    917.78'7970443—dc21   97-43282
                                                 CIP

ISBN 1-55622-570-9
10 9 8 7 6 5 4 3 2 1
9802

All inquiries for volume purchases of this book should be addressed to
Wordware Publishing, Inc., at 2320 Los Rios Blvd., Plano, Texas 75074.
Telephone inquiries may be made by calling:

(214) 423-0090

Contents

Contents

Section Seven
Branson: America's New Music and
Entertainment Capital!

Contents

Contents

Contents

Contents

Section Fourteen
**Great Places To Dine: Restaurants,
Cafes, Bistros, and Taverns**. 195

Contents

Section Fifteen
**Places To Stay: Hotels, Motels, Condos,
Resorts, Inns, and Bed and Breakfasts** 227

Contents

Section Sixteen
Festivals

Test Your Knowledge

1. The town of Branson is located in:
   A. Branson County
   B. Taney County
   C. Missouri County
   D. Stone County
2. The town of Branson is found in which mountain range?
   A. The Rocky Mountains
   B. The Appalachian Mountains
   C. The Ozark Mountains
   D. The Ouachita Mountains
3. The most common rocks found in the Ozark Mountains around Branson are:
   A. Limestone and dolomite
   B. Sandstone and shale
   C. Marble and granite
   D. Quartz and orthoclase
4. The town of Branson is located how many feet above sea level?
   A. 200 feet
   B. 800 feet
   C. 1,600 feet
   D. 2,400 feet
5. The average age of the rocks in the Ozark Mountains is:
   A. 400,000,000 years old
   B. 100,000,000 years old
   C. 50,000 years old
   D. 4,034 years old.
6. In the Ozarks, the words knob and bald refer to:
   A. A bald-headed man
   B. A bald-headed woman

    C. A trail hitch

    D. An elevated bare expanse of rock

7. Early Indian tribes that settled in the Ozarks include:

    A. Apache and Comanche

    B. Sioux and Cheyenne

    C. Kiowa and Arapaho

    D. Osage and Caddo

8. The first permanent settlers in the Branson region of the Ozarks were:

    A. Indians

    B. French

    C. Germans

    D. Italians

9. According to historians, the first white settlers in the Ozarks were:

    A. Welsh and Scots

    B. British and Irish

    C. French and Spanish

    D. Germans and Scandinavians

10. Animals once plentiful but now extinct in the Ozarks include:

    A. Bison and grizzly bears

    B. White-tail deer and raccoons

    C. Opossum and beaver

    D. Red squirrels and gray squirrels

11. The most common bear found in the Ozarks is the:

    A. Black bear

    B. Grizzly bear

    C. Brown bear

    D. Polar bear

12. The Battle of Pea Ridge was fought in what state?

    A. Arkansas

    B. Missouri

    C. Oklahoma

    D. Kansas

13. How many movies have been made of *The Shepherd of the Hills* based on the novel by Harold Bell Wright?
    A. 2
    B. 3
    C. 4
    D. 5
14. The Inspiration Tower at the Shepherd of the Hills Theme Park weighs:
    A. 1,000,000 pounds
    B. 2,000,000 pounds
    C, 3,000,000 pounds
    D. 4,000,000 pounds
15. Branson entertainer Andy Williams' biggest hit was:
    A. Moonlight in Vermont
    B. Moon Over Miami
    C. Moonlight Sonata
    D. Moon River
16. The town of Branson has a population of approximately:
    A. 400,000
    B. 40,000
    C. 4,000
    D. 400
17. Early prehistoric mammals that lived in the Branson area were:
    A. Armadillos
    B. Mastodons and mammoths
    C. Brontosaurus
    D. Tyrannosaurus Rex
18. Among the first crops raised in the Branson area Ozarks was:
    A. Corn
    B. Coffee
    C. Tobacco
    D. Broccoli

19. According to folklore, the early Spanish explorers entered the Ozark Mountains and mined:
    A. Tin and bauxite
    B. Quartz
    C. Gold and silver
    D. Silica
20. Early mining activities by Italian settlers yielded vast quantities of:
    A. Gold
    B. Lead
    C. Silver
    D. Quartz

Answers

1. B
2. C
3. A
4. B
5. A
6. D
7. D
8. A
9. C
10. A
11. A
12. A
13. C
14. C
15. D
16. C
17. B
18. A
19. C
20. B

Branson! Where is It? What is It?

Geographic Location

The town of Branson is located in the rugged Ozark Mountains of Taney County in southwestern Missouri near the Arkansas border. Straddling Highway 65, Branson is a town of less than 4,000 residents. Once a sleepy little village composed of log cabins and small farms, Branson has experienced remarkable growth during the past three decades to become one of the most favored tourist destinations in the United States. Here, one can find some of the nation's foremost musical attractions, theme parks, a wide variety of outdoor recreation of all types for young and old, and some of the finest dining and award-winning restaurants in the region.

Access

Located forty miles south of Springfield, sixty-five miles southeast of Joplin, Missouri, and twenty-five miles north of Harrison, Arkansas, Branson is easily accessible by car, motor home, and tour bus. Highway 65 is the principal travel artery through Branson, but a number of

Branson is located in America's Heartland close to several major cities.

secondary and tertiary roads will bring the traveler into town from rural environments of Missouri and Arkansas.

The Springfield/Branson Airport, located in Springfield, houses terminals for a number of airlines, including American Eagle, Northwest Airlink, Trans World Express, and TWA. At the airport, six rental car companies can provide transportation to Branson. In addition, shuttle services, taxi cabs, and limousine service are available from Springfield to Branson.

A smaller airport, the M. Graham Clark Airport, is located at the College of the Ozarks in Hollister, about two miles south of Branson. Clark Airport is able to accommodate small craft and helicopters. There is one rental car company located at the airport.

Culture

Culturally speaking, Branson, Missouri, overlaps from the frontier days of early and primitive settlement to the high-tech age of today. Manifestations of the region's exciting history are found everywhere, and much of it is expertly preserved so visitors can enjoy it.

As one of the country's premier entertainment and recreation areas, Branson offers most of the facilities found in larger cities, all of it modern and up-to-date.

A visit to the Branson Welcome Center, located at 911 West Highway 76, will provide the traveler with information and brochures on dining, lodging, recreation of all types, and shows.

The Setting

The Environment

It is the opinion of many, visitors and residents alike, that the town of Branson is located in one of the most beautiful and photogenic sections of the western reaches of the Ozark Mountains. Nestled in a gorgeous setting amid impressive limestone outcrops and deep and narrow valleys containing cold-running, fish-filled streams, this popular vacation destination offers most of the amenities and diversions found in a big city along with a giant serving of rural countryside and a generous sprinkling of the distinct Ozark Mountain culture.

The Ozark Mountains that dominate the scenic landscape here are variously called the Ozark Highlands, Ozark Uplift, Ozark Upland, Ozark Plateau, and Ozark Hill Country. Actually an enormous plateau, this geologically uplifted section of crust extends across portions of Missouri, Arkansas, Oklahoma, and a tiny bit of Kansas, covering over 50,000 square miles and extending across at least ninety-three counties.

Historic downtown Branson as seen from the top of Mount Branson

The word Ozark, incidentally, comes from the French *Aux Arc*, which early French explorers applied to a wide bend, or arc, in the Arkansas River far to the south.

Based on differences in geology and topography, the Ozark Mountains have been classified by geologists into a variety of subdivisions. The town of Branson is located on the White River Hills section of the Springfield Plateau, a major division of the Ozark range.

Altitude above sea level in the Ozark Mountains ranges from 400 feet to over 2,500 feet. In Missouri, the tallest Ozark prominence is 1,778. The town of Branson is located at around 800 feet above sea level and is ringed by a number of Ozark crests and ridges.

Though not nearly as high as the Rocky Mountains, their counterparts in the American West, the Ozark Mountains are nevertheless quite spectacular. Their gentle features and tree-covered slopes provide tranquil environments for wildlife, hikers, campers, and sightseers.

The Ozark Mountains stretch across the state of Missouri, Arkansas, and Oklahoma.

The gentle Ozarks, at one time millions of years ago, rivaled the Rockies in altitude, but millennia of erosion have sculpted them into the low, rounded, gentle forms they manifest today.

Geological Origins

The Ozarks have been described by some scientists as America's oldest mountain range, and are composed primarily of limestone and dolomite—sedimentary rocks that were deposited at the bottom of a vast sea approximately 400 million years ago. As a result, a wide variety of fossilized marine shellfish such as brachiopods, pelycy-pods, ammonites, as well as others, have been found in the Ozark rocks, and collectors regularly come to this area to search for museum-quality specimens. Many spectacular fossil discoveries have been made in the Branson area, and accessibility to the fossil-rich locations in the mountains is easy.

The Ozark Mountains are made up primarily of limestone and dolomite rocks. Outcrops such as this can be seen along the highways.

Following a series of tectonic episodes (earthquakes, folding, and volcanic eruptions), which caused the region to be uplifted several thousand feet above the surrounding plains, the Ozarks have subsequently been eroded to lower elevations as a result of the influence of flowing water. The streams and rivers of the region continue to be the most active and apparent erosional force in these mountains, and the deeply cut valleys seen today throughout the region are testimony to their effectiveness.

Volcanic activity, both above and below ground, occurred often during the millions of years of existence of the Ozark Mountains, but ceased long before humans ever occupied the region. As a result of eons of erosion, however, hardly any evidence of volcanic activity can be found today in the Branson area.

The mountains themselves are characterized by bold sedimentary rock bluffs and prominences composed of limestone and dolomite. Bare expanses of rock outcrops are common, especially around Branson, and are called knobs or balds. These balds figure prominently in local place names, as landmarks, and have important historical significance.

One of the most interesting properties of limestone and dolomite rock is solubility. These two types of rock are noted for their capacity to dissolve. Over time, these rocks are susceptible to the solutioning process of water which percolates slowly and inexorably through crevices, joints, cracks, and bedding planes, ultimately giving rise to solution channels, caves, and surface landforms such as sinkholes, some of them quite deep. Numerous impressive caverns can be found in the region, both commercial and wild, and are experienced and enjoyed by thousands of visitors every year (see Section Eleven, Ozark Caverns).

Springs

Springs and underground streams are also common features of cavern-riddled limestone environments, and the Ozark Mountains are noted for an abundance of fresh spring water. Throughout history, a number of the springs found in the area near Branson attracted Indians from as far away as the Great Plains. These Native Americans believed the waters possessed magical curative properties, and used them to treat a variety of infirmities including arthritis, skin problems, cancer, and certain digestive ailments.

The earliest white settlers in the area also believed in the medicinal effects of the waters, and some of the first communities in various parts of the Ozarks, such as Eureka Springs and Siloam Springs, Arkansas, were built around such consistent outflows of water. Since the 1800s, visitors have immersed themselves in these spring waters and drunk thousands of gallons in the hope of curing cancer, arthritis, rheumatism, venereal disease, emphysema, the common cold, and malaise.

Today, several notable Ozark springs still attract hundreds of visitors each year who continue to believe in the reputed healing properties of the waters. However, the waters of many lakes found in the region now cover a number of the springs.

A Geological Mystery?

The Missouri Ozarks are the setting for a curious and ongoing geological controversy. Stretching across several miles of the Ozark landscape can be found a series of six mysterious craters that have confounded experts during the past several years.

A number of prominent geologists are convinced these craters are the remains of ancient volcanic cones. Others, however, scoff at this suggestion and maintain the craters are meteorite impact craters, the result of the simultaneous collision of six meteorites with the earth, all of them striking this region sometime during the prehistoric past.

To date, no definite conclusions have been drawn, and the mystery continues.

Exploration and Settlement

Throughout their history, the Ozark Mountains have been noted for the variety of cultures that have encountered, entered, and settled into these relatively peaceful hills and hollows. In addition to the American Indians who first visited and settled in the area, the Ozarks have seen the comings and goings of Spanish, French, and Americans, all of whom saw promise in this incredibly fascinating land.

Indians

Throughout the years, numerous archeological studies conducted in the Ozark Mountains have yielded a great deal of important and interesting information about the region's first settlers.

It is believed American Indians first entered the Ozark Mountains approximately 14,000 years ago in search of game. According to archeologists, mastodon and mammoth, which once lived in the northern Ozarks, likely furnished a significant portion of their food. With the abundance of game and fresh water found here, the Indians eventually moved into the region and established permanent settlements. Over time, they grew less dependent on hunting and became more involved in pursuing a primitive type of agriculture along the fertile river bottoms. Villages were generally small and not very plentiful.

Among the tribes that eventually came to live in the Ozark Mountains were the Osage, Illinois, Caddo, and Quapaw. The Osage occupied most of the western and interior portions of the range where the town of Branson is found today.

By 1700 regular trade with French trappers became common, and the Indian cultures began to undergo critical change. As more and more whites entered the region, the Indians were gradually dispossessed and removed to reserved lands further west in what is now the state of Oklahoma.

By 1804, following the Louisiana Purchase, several eastern tribes, most notably the Kickapoos, moved into the Ozark Mountains. In 1808 the Osages finally ceded their claims to a large portion of the Ozarks. Soon, Cherokees, Shawnees, Peorias, Piankashaws, and Delawares began moving in. By the mid-1820s, approximately 8,000 Algonquians and 6,000 Cherokees inhabited southwestern Missouri and northwestern Arkansas.

Cherokees from Georgia, South Carolina, and Tennessee voluntarily arrived in the Ozarks long before the infamous Trail of Tears, the formal displacement of several southeastern tribes that occurred during the early to mid-1830s. Once in their new home, these early Cherokees established excellent farms and were reported to have raised fine horses. Eventually, they too were displaced by white settlers who wanted the land, and most of the Indians were moved to Indian Territory.

Indian settlement in the Ozarks had very little impact on the mountain landscape. They lived a relatively primitive existence and were engaged primarily in a subsistence level hunting-gathering-farming economy. Beans, corn, squash, and pumpkins were grown along the river bottoms. Wild game, including deer, bear, raccoon, and a variety of birds, rounded out their diet.

Homes were constructed of native materials and consisted primarily of round or oblong huts made from poles and covered with buffalo hides or a thatch of reeds, cattails, and other materials.

Spanish

Historians agree that portions of the Ozark Mountains were visited and explored by the Spaniards under the leadership of Hernando DeSoto during the 1540s. Numerous tales of the discovery and mining of rich deposits of gold and silver by the Spanish endure to this day (see Section Five, Folklore of the Ozarks). It is believed that continued pressure from the area Indians, along with pressing political problems with Spain, caused the Spanish to ultimately abandon the area. Before they left, it is reported they sealed up many of the richest mines and buried millions of dollars' worth of treasure. Modern day treasure hunters continue to visit the Ozark Mountains to search for several of these lost bonanzas and buried treasures still believed to exist here.

French

The region now known as the Ozark Mountains was once part of the French Province of Louisiana, and the French were the first whites to explore and occupy the area in significant numbers. During the mid to late 1600s and early 1700s, the French established settlements along the Mississippi and Missouri Rivers and engaged in mining, fur trapping, agriculture, and trade with the Indians. Inspired by tales of large deposits of gold and silver in the western Ozarks, the French entered the region in the hope of discovering some valuable ore. While some small amounts of silver and gold were found, most of the mining activities during this period were associated with the extraction of lead, which was in great demand for bullets on this frontier.

Americans

The first American immigrants into the Ozark Mountains were Southerners, principally of Scotch-Irish decent, and mostly poor. The majority of the early arrivals came from the upper south regions of Tennessee, North Carolina, Virginia, Pennsylvania, and Kentucky.

Initially, settlement consisted of detached farms or small hamlets along rivers and creeks. The river bottom deposits of relatively fertile soil were an important factor in getting agriculture established. In time, some farming was moved to the uplands where corn and wheat were grown. The extremely rugged hills and numerous rock outcrops, however, made farming difficult in the western Ozarks. In spite of that, the hardy pioneers persevered and ultimately succeeded in carving out a decent living here.

Prior to the 1950s, Branson, along with the surrounding environment, was considered a rather remote location, isolated somewhat from larger centers of population. Traditional technologies dominated, and the residents expressed a certain disdain for city life along with an overt suspicion of outsiders. Conservative in nature, they built their own cabins out of logs, made most of their own furniture, and treated the sick with traditional folk remedies.

The residents here coaxed meager crops from the thin soils of the hillsides and river bottoms, and supplemented their diets with wild game such as deer, elk, turkey, dove, quail, and bear. Catfish, bass, bream, and crappies caught in the local streams also provided variety to their diet.

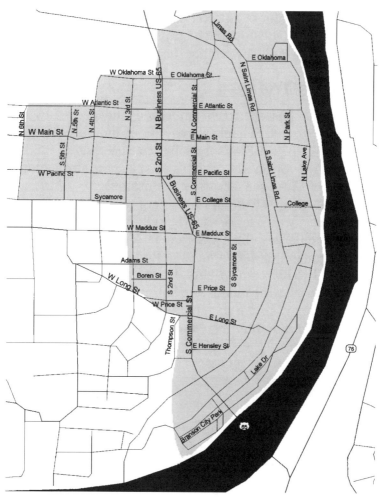

Historic downtown Branson on the shores of Lake Taneycomo

Fundamentalist religion dominated in the Ozarks. Church attendance was regular and highly encouraged, and brush arbor revivals and river baptisms were common. Quite often, community and family activities revolved around the church.

15

In 1881 businessman Reuben Branson allowed a post office to be established in the tiny country store he operated, thus formally providing the town with its name.

Branson Today

As time passed, roads improved and access to the region increased. Schools were built, economies changed, and rising expectations relative to the quality of life caused some dramatic changes in the heretofore-simple lifestyle of these conservative mountaineers.

Soon, waves of immigrants were arriving, and these newcomers were more liberal, educated, progressive-minded souls who brought innovation and investment. Soon Branson became more and more cosmopolitan. Eventually, there was a shift from the traditional technologies to growing businesses in tourism and recreation.

Branson was changing, but few people could have predicted how far it would go and what it would eventually become—one of the most prominent music, entertainment, and vacation centers of the United States!

History of the Branson Area

Given the comparatively small population, coupled with the relative remoteness and isolation of its location for several generations, the town of Branson and the surrounding area boasts a remarkably rich and lively history, one that impacted heavily on the region and the culture at the time and has influenced the attraction and development of this region today.

Many travelers into and through this part of the Ozarks are aware of Harold Bell Wright's turn-of-the-century novel *The Shepherd of the Hills*, a 1907 publication that introduced most of America to the Ozark Mountains and environs. Few who drive along these Ozark roads and explore the picturesque mountains and valleys, however, are aware of the multitude of significant historical events related to the Civil War that occurred here, or of the formation and role of the secret society called the Bald Knobbers, or of the impact of the coming of the railroad.

Civil War

By the time the Civil War was well under way throughout much of the American South, Branson, Missouri, and the neighboring Ozark Mountains were still sparsely settled. It was only after the passage of several months that many who lived in this area were even aware a war was being conducted. Though it did not seem likely that the conflict raging hundreds of miles to the east could touch this somewhat remote environment, the War did, in fact, land in southwestern Missouri with great unanticipated force, and it impacted heavily on the region.

A few miles to the north of Branson, the Battle of Wilson's Creek was fought during the early stages of the War on 10 August 1861. Union troops, commanded by General Nathaniel Lyon, encountered the General Sterling Price-led Rebel forces in one of the most violent and bloody clashes west of the Mississippi River. By battle's end, the Confederates claimed a victory, but 2,330 dead soldiers lay on the ground. Among them was General Lyon himself, the first Yankee general to be killed in the War Between the States. The victory was short-lived, however, for the Union regained control of the region one-and-a-half years later.

Between March 6 and March 8, 1862, another significant battle was fought at Pea Ridge, Arkansas, located some sixty miles southwest of Branson. This time, the Union triumphed over a Confederate force nearly double in size, an army which included approximately 1,000 Indian troops—Cherokees, Choctaws, Chickasaws, Creeks, and Seminoles.

Major Civil War battles were the exception, and not the rule, in the Ozarks. Despite the actions at Wilson's Creek and Pea Ridge, most of the confrontations in these mountains involved small bands of raiders and guerrillas bushwhacking and otherwise harassing the armies.

Southwestern Missouri was located between the Confederate allegiances of Arkansas to the South and the anti-slavery attitudes of Kansas to the west. Both Union and Confederate raiders traveled back and forth while attempting to hamper enemy movements, and confrontations often occurred in the middle region consisting primarily of the Ozark Mountains. Unfortunately, around this time bandits, horse and cattle thieves, and other badmen used the war as an opportunity to attack scattered settlements and farms in the Ozarks. Because of the roaming and raiding bands of soldiers, guerillas, and outlaws, tiny settlements like Branson often bore the brunt of hostile activities.

One of the most notorious outlaws of this time was Missourian Alf Bolin, a Stone Countian who swore allegiance neither to North nor South. Often described as a madman, Bolin, leading a gang numbering up to thirty killers and robbers, terrorized, robbed, and killed throughout the Branson Ozarks. It was once reported that the Alf Bolin Gang was responsible for over fifty murders!

So feared and dangerous was Bolin that the Union forces eventually offered a $5,000 reward for the outlaw. History and folklore note that several men made an attempt to collect the reward but were killed. It has also been told that those who tried to take Bolin's life suffered horrible tortures before they were finally put to death. Their bodies were often hung from or nailed to trees as a warning to others who would try to collect the reward.

It was a Confederate sympathizer who helped put an end to Bolin's criminal career. Robert Foster, a prisoner at the Union army camp at Springfield, offered to capture or kill Bolin in exchange for his freedom. Foster explained that his cabin was located only a few miles from Bolin's hideout, and he felt certain he could lure the outlaw into his home where he could be taken.

The Federals liked Foster's idea, but decided to keep him confined in the prison. Instead, Corporal Z.E. Thomas of the Iowa Volunteer Cavalry was sent, alone, to the Foster cabin.

Corporal Thomas remained as a guest in the Foster cabin, located a few miles east of Branson. According to the plan that was devised, Mrs. Foster invited Bolin to the residence ostensibly to sell him some cattle. Bolin arrived a few days later and was introduced to Thomas, who identified himself as an escaped Confederate soldier. When Bolin briefly turned his back to light his pipe from the fireplace, Thomas hit the outlaw in the head with a plow handle and knocked him unconscious. Believing Bolin was dead, Thomas dragged him to the barn and covered him with hay and other materials. As Thomas was saddling his horse, Bolin regained consciousness and attempted to stand. Turning quickly, Thomas drew his cap and ball pistol and shot a bullet through the heart of the outlaw, ending his life forever.

Thomas left immediately for Union headquarters in Springfield and returned at dawn the following day with a wagon and a contingent of twenty-five cavalrymen. Bolin's corpse was thrown into the back of the wagon to be returned to Springfield.

While Thomas was leading the party back to Springfield as proof of the outlaw's death, angry Ozarkians near the town of Forsyth approached the wagon and, while Thomas was distracted, jumped into it and chopped the outlaw's head off in revenge for his dastardly deeds. After burying the headless body, Thomas placed the severed head in a gunnysack and proceeded on toward Springfield. In the town of Ozark, however, another mob approached the wagon and secured the head. After mounting it on a long pole, they erected it on the courthouse lawn where they threw rocks at it all day. When the head finally reached Springfield, it was little more than a skull covered with dry, stretched skin.

As a result of the killing of Alf Bolin, Foster was granted a pardon and Thomas was rewarded with a commission as a second lieutenant and a $5,000 reward. Thomas split the reward with Foster.

The tale of Alf Bolin does not end with his death. His ghost, according to many, still haunts the Ozarks (see Section Five, Folklore of the Ozarks).

The Bald Knobbers

The Ozarks in and around Branson were at one time best known as the territory of the Bald Knobbers, a night-riding terrorist group responsible for the killing of dozens and the beatings and evictions of hundreds more.

The Bald Knobbers were not the only secret society to be associated with the Ozarks. There were at least four others: The Anti-Horsethief Association, the Regulators, a curious group called the Honest Men's League, and an organization called the Slickers, who beat offenders with slim hickory switches, or "slicks."

On the night of April 5, 1885, a group of men, all masked and heavily armed, met on top of Snapp Bald. A bald is a bare, open patch of exposed rock with little or no vegetation. Snapp Bald offered remoteness and protection for the clandestine gathering, and the surrounding countryside could easily be watched from the ridges.

On this night, the men gathered atop the bald were determined to exact their own brand of justice on neighbors they believed to be breaking the law and/or the moral codes of the community. Offenders included everyone from horse thieves to men who beat their wives. Originally, this group was called the Law and Order League, but as a result of the geographic location where it held its secret meetings, they eventually became known locally as the Bald Knobbers. The Bald Knobbers were men who claimed to be tired of the growing number of killings and other crimes, as well as a number of other moral lapses in the region. They also stated concern about the lack of adequate law enforcement and decided to take matters, once and for all, into their own hands.

When a malefactor was identified, the Bald Knobbers would ride to his home, pull him from the house, inform him of his crimes, and punish him. Punishment ranged from whippings to hanging.

The history of the Bald Knobbers is closely related to the beginnings of the town of Branson. Shortly after Branson became established in 1881, an investor named Nat McKinney purchased just over 250 acres of land fronting the White River near where Lake Taneycomo is located today. McKinney eagerly looked forward to the day Branson became a prosperous town and participating in its growth, but he was becoming more and more discouraged at the lawlessness that permeated the valley.

McKinney, a self-styled preacher who carried pistols into his church, was a large man (six-and-a-half-feet tall, weighing over 300 pounds, ham-sized arms, and a huge handlebar moustache!). He also had a mean disposition. History records he was a bare-knuckles fighter of some renown both in the Union army and after he was discharged and moved to Missouri.

Nat McKinney was the principal motivating force in the formation of the Bald Knobbers.

The Bald Knobbers consisted of both former Union and Confederate soldiers but for the most part sided with Union policies and philosophies. Among the members were farmers, businessmen, and several preachers.

Employing vigilante justice, the Bald Knobbers exacted their brand of justice throughout the Taney County countryside for the next three years. It is estimated that the membership soared to as many as 1,000 men. Thieves and murderers were regularly lynched, and those accused and found guilty of lesser crimes were horsewhipped or driven out of town. Even women thought to be unfaithful were pulled from their beds, tied to trees, and mercilessly whipped. Before the Bald Knobbers ceased their reign of justice, records indicate that at least thirty men and four women died at their hands, and hundreds more were chased from their homes by these nightriders.

Eventually, the Bald Knobbers began to inspire as much fear as did the real criminals. As a result, an Anti-Bald Knobbers Society was formed, which appealed for help from Missouri Governor John S. Marmaduke. Marmaduke reacted to the citizens' concern by sending Adjutant General J.C. Jamison to southwestern Missouri to rid the environment of the Bald Knobbers. Jamison had varied military experience and had served in the Civil War with General Sterling Price. Jamison also commanded the state militia, thus he was able to call up an impressive force of men when and if necessary.

On arriving in Branson, Jamison announced in no uncertain terms to one and all that he was giving the Bald Knobbers just twenty-four hours to disband or the state militia would be brought in. McKinney responded by requesting a forty-eight-hour delay, and the general agreed.

With this pronouncement, the activities of Bald Knobbers gradually came to an end. Though sporadic raids were conducted throughout the region during the next few months, there was a noticeable decrease in violence in Taney County.

With the power and influence of the Bald Knobbers all but gone, several attempts were made on the life of Nat McKinney as well as other prominent members.

Instead of laying low or leaving town, McKinney, who many believed controlled local elections, decided instead to run for State Representative. Threats on his life continued, and it was reported that people openly prayed for McKinney's death during church services. On August 20,

1888, McKinney was shot dead in Kirbyville by one Billy Miles, a killing that was ultimately ruled self-defense.

For several years after the reign of terror unleashed on the Ozarks by the Bald Knobbers and the subsequent bad press in national newspapers, the region was shunned by potential settlers and investors, and many feared the once-quiet little community of Branson would shrivel up and die.

But the town would not die, and relief was not far away. It came in the form of the railroad.

The Railroad

In 1901 railroad surveyors entered the still somewhat secluded Ozarks around Branson and undertook the task of laying out a route that eventually became known as the White River Railway. Five years later, in 1906, the first train chugged through this sleepy Ozark town and brought with it the promise of an economic boom.

With the railroad came linkage with major cities and bigger markets for area resources. Among the resources identified in the Branson area were the forests—the first-growth pines and hardwoods. Some of this timber was used for railroad ties during the initial laying of the track through the area, and hundreds of workers were employed. Later, the forests were harvested for woods that were eventually used in the manufacture of pencils and barrel staves.

With the marketing of the area timber, along with some regionally produced fruits and vegetables, outsiders were gradually learning more and more about this quiet little part of southwestern Missouri. Memories of the violence associated with the Bald Knobbers had dimmed significantly, and people from the bigger cities such as St. Louis, Kansas City, Des Moines, and even Chicago began visiting the area to fish in the clear streams. In many cases, they rode the trains to Branson.

Others learned about the existence of several spectacular caves found in the region and came to explore them, while many arrived to simply enjoy the beauty and splendor of the Ozarks.

With the passage of a few years, the coming of the railroad was eventually responsible for putting Branson on the map as a growing tourist destination.

The Shepherd of the Hills

If the coming of the railroads started the town of Branson toward boom times, the publication of the widely acclaimed book *The Shepherd of the Hills* shifted the momentum into a higher gear. Published in 1907, *The Shepherd of the Hills* introduced readers across the country to the special and colorful people and environs of the Ozark Mountains and Branson. Expertly employing Ozark Mountain dialect, this spirited, action-packed, and truly romantic book enthralled, and continues to enthrall, millions.

Author Harold Bell Wright, a minister, arrived in the Branson Ozarks during the 1890s and lived a rather spartan life in a small camp on the farm of J.K. Ross. Captivated by the hills and the people, Wright began to craft his novel, basing the characters on local folk.

On publication, *The Shepherd of the Hills* surged to best seller, and the book generated hordes of visitors to this still somewhat tiny community. For a time, visitors by the score flocked to Branson daily to see, feel, and touch the region that served as the book's setting.

Initially, Branson residents didn't know what to make of the flocks of visitors. J.K. Ross and his wife, Anna (who served as the inspirations for the book's characters Old Matt and Aunt Ollie), were unable to endure the crowds of out-of-towners ranging across their farm, and finally moved away.

Lizzie McDaniel, whose father was a prominent Springfield banker, purchased the Ross property, restored the original home, and furnished it with authentic pieces. In time, she constructed a new home for herself not far away. McDaniel devoted the rest of her life to maintaining the old homestead, collecting information and genealogy on the Ross family, and producing the first outdoor dramas based on Harold Bell Wright's book.

On McDaniel's death, her property was willed to the Branson Civic League on the condition that it continue the performances. Several years later, the League sold the property to Dr. Bruce Trimble. Trimble, a scholar and avid fan of Wright, converted the McDaniel home into a museum in order to display the many manifestations of the culture and literature of the Ozarks.

After Trimble's death in 1957, his widow, Mary, and his son, Mark, teamed with a man named Shad Heller to create a theater in which to present *The Shepherd of the Hills* as a regular stage production. Heller wrote the play, and in 1960 the curtain was raised on the first performance in what was then called the Old Mill Theater. The local Mabe brothers served as musicians in the play and eventually took their new professional stage name, the Baldknobbers, from their role.

The play is still performed today, and the Shepherd of the Hills theme park is one of Branson's foremost attractions (see Section Eight, Theme Parks).

Fishing

In 1913 Branson's Powersite Dam backed up the waters of White River to create Lake Taneycomo. Before the dam was constructed, the flow of the White River ranged from regular to unpredictable. In addition to the new lake, the dam provided hydroelectric power.

Long a popular fishing destination, Branson and Lake Taneycomo (a combination of the words Taney, County, and Missouri) proved quite inviting to a growing number of sportsmen. In addition to fishing, the new lake was suitable for boating and other water sports. Resort-type areas such as Rockaway Beach were developed on the lakeshore, and the lake gradually lured more and more vacationers from around the country.

The popularity of the region became attractive to former actors and singers, many of whom had vaudeville experience and who decided to launch second careers at the new resorts. The imported music, along with the homegrown strains of folk tunes, provided a wide variety of entertainment offerings for visitors.

Growth of Tourism

The combination of idyllic mountain life, recreational opportunities manifested by the lake, the growing number of resorts, and the burgeoning musical offerings led many to believe Branson had the potential for an even greater economic boom. Magazine publisher Ernest Rayburn wrote in *Arcadian Life* that Americans are entering a period of vast and intense recreational development in the Ozarks, an intensity that is gaining momentum. "Branson," he stated, "is the ideal center for this vast activity."

Music

As more and more music rang from the Ozark hills around Branson, members of two of the town's families decided to capitalize on the wide and growing appeal. In 1959 the Mabe brothers leased a room in the Branson City Hall where they produced a weekly musical show called the Baldknobbers Hillbilly Jamboree, much to the delight of visiting customers.

One year later, the Shepherd of the Hills outdoor theater opened with the production of the Harold Bell Wright play along with other musical performances. In 1967 Lloyd Presley, observing the success of the Baldknobbers musical program, opened the Presley Family Music Show on Highway 76. The following year, the Baldknobbers moved from City Hall to another location on the same highway just a few doors down from the Presleys.

The next few years saw the establishment of a growing number of music halls and theaters, and there soon followed an expanding reputation of Branson as the nation's new center for country music. Branson truly leaped into the national limelight, however, when country-western music performer and television star Roy Clark moved to town to open his theater in 1983. At that point, the music boom became a full-fledged explosion.

Today, Branson claims more musical performances per day than any other place in the United States. With over forty locations featuring singing and dancing from the breakfast hour to well past midnight, the entertainment opportunities seem endless (see Section Seven, Branson: America's New Music and Entertainment Capital).

Folklore of the Ozarks: Lost Mines, Buried Treasures, Ghosts, and Monsters

As much as any other region in the United States, the Ozark Mountains are home to a great deal of rich and colorful lore and legend. Handed down from generation to generation via the oral tradition, the fascinating lore provided by Ozarkers includes tales of lost mines and buried treasures, ghosts, and monsters. Here are some of the more prominent and popular stories to come out of these mountains.

Lost Mine

Few locations of legendary buried treasure in the Ozarks have received as much attention as the mysterious cave located just a few short miles northwest of Branson at Reeds Spring, Stone County.

There is little disagreement among researchers that a tremendous wealth in gold and silver lies concealed deep within this cavern. Many have inquired why more effort is not made to retrieve it. Many attempts have been made, but a succession of cave-ins and excavation attempts have only served to rearrange the interior passageways and chambers such that they now bear little resemblance to the site the Spaniards selected over four hundred years ago for caching a great fortune in gold and silver ingots.

In recent years, a section of the cavern was opened for tourists who regularly visit this fascinating location. This particular Spanish treasure cave differs little from other caverns in the area, but over one hundred years ago it was the center of one of the most intensive treasure hunts that ever took place in the Ozarks.

Though the exact date is uncertain, most people believe the first formal search for the treasure began in 1888 when an aged man appeared one day in the town of Joplin looking for work. He was described as dark and Mediterranean-looking, probably a Spaniard. He eventually secured a nighttime job mopping out one of the local taverns. He had not been employed long when he was felled by a serious illness, probably tuberculosis. Two Joplin residents, who also happened to be patrons of the tavern in which the old man worked, took pity on him, brought him to their room at a nearby hotel, and tended to his ailment to the best of their ability. When the old fellow grew progressively worse, a physician was finally brought to the room. After examining the Spaniard, the doctor proclaimed he was dying and had very little time left.

After the doctor left, the old man summoned his two new friends to the bedside. He weakly waved an arm toward his small pile of modest belongings in the corner of the room and told the men he wanted them to have all of his money and possessions in gratitude for their care. The two friends sat up the entire night with the old man, but by dawn he was dead.

Later that day when the men examined the old Spaniard's belongings they found only a few coins, barely enough for a decent burial. The meager garments he owned were little more than rags, and the men elected to throw them away. As they gathered up the old clothes, a rolled parchment fell from the inside of a worn, tattered coat. On examining it, the two men were stunned to discover a map sketched onto the vellum, a map with numerous symbols and notations in Spanish. Employing their rudimentary knowledge of the language, they interpreted an amazing story from the old chart.

Sometime during the sixteenth century, according to the parchment, a group of Spanish soldiers and laborers under the command of Hernando DeSoto's officers were driving a twenty-mule pack train carrying loads of gold and silver ingots through the Ozarks. The ore had been dug from mines far to the southwest in Texas and was being transported to a location on the Mississippi River where it was to be loaded onto flatboats, floated to the Gulf of Mexico, and then shipped to Spain on an awaiting galleon.

As the Spaniards led the pack train along the winding trail through the Ozarks, they searched for more signs of valuable ore. During an extended encampment intended to rest men and horses in a location near what is now the town of Reeds Spring, one of the Spaniards discovered a vein of silver in a deep cave. Impressed with the richness of the ore, the leader of the group gave orders to commence mining immediately.

A crude log fort was hastily constructed as protection against the coming winter and the potential of marauding Indians. The extraction of the silver proceeded smoothly, but Indian attacks occurred with increasing frequency and several men were killed. Eventually, the Spaniards felt their lives were in serious danger and they couldn't hold out much longer. They decided to hide the gold and quit the area until sometime in the future when it might be safe to return. They also concealed the entrance to the cave before departing.

After interpreting the old treasure map, the two friends decided that the Spaniard had come into the Ozarks in search of the long-lost treasure cache and mine, but apparently was never able to locate it.

Several weeks after the burial of the Spaniard, the two men who cared for him during his final days undertook a search for the cave described on the parchment. According to the description, the cave was supposed to be located in a remote part of Stone County. The map indicated the search was to begin near three large trees arranged in a triangle. Each of the trees was identified as having crescent-shaped markings carved into the trunk. The markings supposedly pointed to the site of the fort constructed by the Spanish soldiers, a location that was supposed to be at the base of an overhanging limestone bluff. Nearby, along the base of the same bluff, according to the map, was the entrance of the treasure cave.

The map indicated the cave entrance was covered and disguised to look exactly like the rest of the bluff. To gain entrance to the cave a barrier had to be removed, exposing a low, narrow opening. Once inside, however, the cave was described as being large enough for a tall person to stand. The passageway extended deep into the bluff for over half a mile to where the ingots were stacked. As one explored the passageways, one would pass through thirteen large chambers, each containing impressive cavern formations. At the fourteenth and final chamber, said the map, one would find the cache of gold and silver ingots hidden there by the Spaniards.

The two men searched for the three large trees arranged in a triangle but were never able to locate them. For two years, when time permitted, they searched the area in the hope of discovering some telltale sign that would lead them to the treasure cave. Finally, after investing two years and a great deal of money and energy in a fruitless search, they gave up and concluded that the map must have been a hoax. They eventually turned the parchment over to a Webb City, Missouri, newspaper, which printed a copy of it in 1890.

A few months later, one of the newspapers came into the possession of a Stone County resident named J.J. Mease. Mease was no stranger to gold; he had hoped to strike it rich during the California Gold Rush of 1849 but ultimately came away with nothing. Discouraged, he returned to his Ozark homeland, but his dream of someday finding gold remained very much alive.

Mease prospected for gold and silver throughout the Stone County Ozarks for many years prior to encountering the copy of the map. Following promising leads, he opened several shafts he believed would lead to valuable ore, but wealth continued to elude him.

Mease was as familiar with the terrain in Stone County as anyone was, and when he read the description of the old Spanish cave in the newspaper, he was convinced he knew the location. He contacted a friend named H.R. Brewer, and together the two men undertook a systematic search for the cave.

One day during the summer of 1894, Mease and Brewer found the three large trees, each manifesting barely perceptible crescent-shaped blazes on the trunks. Following the signs on the trees, the men finally came to a high, overhanging limestone bluff. Near one end of a deeply recessed base of the bluff, they found the rotted remains of several large logs and deduced they must have been part of the fort described on the map.

The men observed that the fort had been situated in an ideal site—the overhanging bluff afforded protection from the weather and the position was quite defensible against Indian attack. Several springs gushing clear, cool water were found nearby.

Further examination of the bluff from one end to the other, however, revealed no evidence of an entrance to a cave! Over and over again Mease and Brewer searched back and forth along the rock wall, and each time they came away perplexed. According to the map and the evidence, this had to be the correct site, but they could find nothing.

Mease and Brewer eventually enlisted the help of neighbors, and soon nearly a dozen men were combing the area in search of the cave. One afternoon, one of the men, H.O. Bruffet, was idly digging in the soil along the face of the bluff that had been examined at least a dozen times. Approximately one foot below the surface, Bruffet unearthed a copper bowl and showed it to Mease. After cleaning most of the dirt from the vessel, Mease discerned several Spanish symbols engraved on it. On a hunch, the men continued digging into the ground where the bowl had been found. After removing about three feet of dirt, they made an astounding discovery—under the dirt that had covered it for four centuries was a large, flat stone slab set upright against the base of the cliff. On the face of the stone were carved many of the same symbols found on the old parchment map!

During the entire search, it never occurred to the men that the cave's entrance lay just below the very surface they walked over. The level of the ground at the base of the cliff had been raised to conceal the entrance!

With considerable effort, several of the workers hammered the large stone into smaller pieces and carried them away. Behind the obstacle, they discovered the low, narrow opening to a cave. Just within the small entrance, they found several piles of ashes and charcoal, suggesting human use or occupation in the past. Just beyond the piles of ashes, the floor of the cave dropped abruptly for a dozen feet before it leveled out again. Three men were lowered by rope to the bottom of the dangerous drop, where they encountered three skeletons. Among the bones were found odd pieces of metal that the men decided were parts of Spanish armor.

In addition, lying among the bones and artifacts was an ancient mold made of porcelain that was used to form ingots. The unusually large mold was six inches deep and approximately two and a half feet long. The inside of the mold was coated with a thin film of silver and apparently once served as a form for fashioning ingots.

Along one side of the cavern wall at the bottom of the drop were several more inscriptions similar to the ones found on the stone slab and the map. Convinced that this was indeed the legendary cave that held the long-hidden Spanish treasure, the men agreed to form a company to remove the hoard and split the wealth equally. One of the workers, C.C. Bush, volunteered to travel to Galena, the nearest settlement of any significant size, and obtain a formal deed to the land on which the cave was located. As it turned out, the land was already owned by the Frisco Railway, which agreed to sell it to the group for only three dollars an acre. The men all contributed equally and purchased several acres of the surrounding land.

One week later as the group began clearing away the soil and enlarging the opening to the cave, a young man arrived in the locale making inquires about the digging. He was tall and well dressed in the manner of an attorney. His skin was olive-colored and he spoke with a distinct Spanish accent. After querying area residents for several days about the ongoing excavation, he finally appeared at the cave. When introductions had been made, the newcomer came quickly to the point of his visit and made an offer of $1,000 for the deed to the land on which the excavation was taking place.

The men refused to sell. They believed they were on the threshold of finding and retrieving the Spanish treasure, and the appearance of the young Spaniard offering them a large amount of money convinced them that something of value was certainly to be found inside the cave. Mease and Brewer became friendly with the newcomer and eventually learned his reasons for wanting to purchase the property.

The Spaniard possessed an ancient map similar to the one that had been found many years earlier among the belongings of the dead man in Joplin. Like the other map, it also told of the twenty mule-loads of gold and silver, the fourteen chambers in the cave, and the existence of a thick vein of almost pure silver that was mined and smelted by DeSoto's men nearly four hundred years earlier.

The young Spaniard continued to make offers to the men, but they were all refused. The newcomer finally left the area quietly and was never seen there again.

Once the opening of the cave had been enlarged and the hazard of the sudden drop overcome, the group entered the passageway carrying torches and digging tools. Almost immediately they encountered problems. The floor of the cavern was extremely difficult to traverse. Large chunks of rock had fallen from the fractured roof and blocked passage throughout. Water dripped continuously from the ceiling, making the footing slippery. The way through the cave was crooked and replete with sudden drops and rises, and it was only with great difficulty that the men were able to make any progress at all.

The first day of searching took almost fourteen hours and saw the discovery of only the first three of the chambers. One of the workers suffered a broken leg and had to be carried out.

On and on the workers pushed—crawling, walking, climbing, and sliding. Finally, they passed the thirteenth chamber. Spurred on by the anticipation of finding great wealth at the next turn in the dark passageway, they crawled forward only to encounter their greatest disappointment. When they arrived at what was to have been the fourteenth chamber, they discovered it had been effectively sealed by a huge cave-in that left thousands of tons of rock blocking the entrance.

Armed with only picks and shovels, the men began digging into the rubble, but it soon became obvious they were unequal to the task. The mass of rock that stood between them and the treasure would take months, perhaps years, to remove by hand. Discouraged, the men slowly made their way back to the surface to report their disappointment.

After numerous discussions, the investors decided that whatever treasure might lie hidden deep within the inaccessible fourteenth chamber was not worth the effort it would require to excavate. The project was abandoned and the company dissolved, and all returned to their homes, farms, and businesses.

The dream of finding the hidden wealth, however, did not die in one of the workers. Frank Mease, the son of J.J. Mease, was only a young boy at the time of the excavation. Frank Mease participated in the digging as enthusiastically as any of the men, doing far more than his fair share of the work. He, more than any of the others, was terribly disappointed when it was announced that the project was to be abandoned.

Like his father, young Mease nurtured a dream of wealth. As he grew to manhood he continued to nourish his dream, a dream that someday he would be the one to break into that mysterious fourteenth chamber and find the ancient Spanish fortune.

Frank Mease decided to approach the problem of finding the treasure differently. He decided the task of removing the tons of rock debris could be made simpler if lights and power were available to the men working below the surface. Heretofore, tallow candles and grass torches had supplied the only light, and Mease believed there was a better way.

He observed that a swiftly flowing stream paralleled the main passageway through the cave. In order to use the energy of the flowing water, he constructed a flume that directed the stream to an area where he placed a waterwheel. The wheel, turned by the stream's current, activated a generator that provided electricity for the workers in the cave.

Once Mease had strung electric lights throughout most of the passageways and up to the thirteenth chamber, he examined the possibilities of directing some of the flowing water so that it would remove and carry away much of the rock and debris blocking the entrance to the treasure chamber.

As he was making arrangements to begin construction of his laborsaving idea, misfortune befell the inventive Mease. A huge portion of the cavern roof gave way, and thousands of tons of weakened and crumbling limestone crashed to the floor, making passage beyond the third chamber impossible!

With the sudden cave-in, months of planning and labor were negated. After examining the disaster, Mease decided it would be impossible to penetrate the new obstacle. Being an enterprising man, however, he attempted to make the best of the unfortunate situation. Advertising the cave as the Lost Spanish Treasure Cave, he graded a good road from nearby Highway 65 and charged tourists a small admission to visit the cave entrance where he related the story of the lost treasure. As he profited from this enterprise, he built a gas station and hotel at the intersection of the dirt road and the highway.

Given the existing research, the available evidence, and the huge investment in time and energy of many men, there seems to be little doubt that a great fortune in

Spanish gold and silver does exist deep inside the limestone bluff near Branson. Several experts on caverns in the Missouri Ozarks claim the Spanish treasure cave is most likely part of an extensive cavern system that runs for several miles below the surface. For many years, people have searched for a passageway from other caves into this particular system, one that might connect with the blocked fourteenth chamber of the treasure cave.

Others have maintained that when the Spaniards hid the treasure deep in the cave they placed a curse on it. The curse provided for disaster to befall any who would attempt to retrieve the great treasure except for the rightful heirs. If one believes in such curses, one must assume that the curse is still in effect.

Lost Treasure

Table Rock Lake, a popular destination with tourists and fishermen, is located just to the west of Branson. Few people who fish, boat, and water ski on this beautiful Ozark lake are aware that, just below the surface, lies an incredible lost fortune in gold coins.

Alonzus Hall was one of several notorious outlaws who roamed, robbed, and murdered throughout much of the Ozarks near Branson during the Civil War. Hall has been described as handsome and tall with deep blue eyes and a charming smile. A charismatic person, Hall had little trouble making friends, and he was a favorite of the ladies in any settlement he visited. Hall also found it easy to convince men to join him for his plundering and killing sprees throughout this part of the mountain range.

One spate of criminal activity led to Hall's undoing and eventually cost him his life. Before he died, however, Hall admitted to burying a large fortune in gold coins, a fortune that still lies hidden today in a small cave that is now located beneath the waters of Table Rock Lake only a short distance from Branson.

Alonzus Hall and his gang were well known and feared throughout much of the Ozarks. They ranged primarily from just north of Springfield south to the Arkansas border. Because law enforcement was virtually nonexistent during that time in this wild land, the Hall gang raided and pillaged at will, spreading terror throughout the otherwise peaceful and quiet ridges and valleys.

Early in April 1862, the gang was particularly active, with the intrepid Hall leading six cutthroats into the settlement of Centralia, Missouri, and robbing the bank of $52,000 in gold coin. Riding from town, the outlaws escaped southward into the hills. Townsfolk were reluctant to pursue the well-armed and desperate outlaws into the wild, isolated regions where the criminals knew every trail and hiding place.

As the outlaws rode south, they stopped at two small farmsteads. After asking for and receiving food for themselves and for their horses, they robbed each of the farmers and then rode deeper into the mountains.

Captain W.F. McCullough was in command of a company of Union soldiers temporarily encamped near the Frisco railroad tracks about twenty-five miles west of Springfield when he received word of the bank robbery at Centralia. McCullough had been following the Hall gang for several months and was now ordered to search for them and to try to capture the outlaws at any cost.

On the day following the bank robbery, McCullough received word that the Alonzus Hall gang had been seen traveling south along the old Wilderness Road and were last spotted in Greene County. He immediately ordered his men to pursue the bandits. The soldiers rode twelve hours straight without a break, hoping to overtake the outlaws in the next day or two. The trail led the soldiers through Greene County, into Christian County, and finally into Stone County and the White River.

On the evening of the second day, one of the army scouts reported to McCullough that he had spotted the outlaws camped under a ledge near the bank of the White River about a mile away. At the same time, one of the outlaws who had been posted as a lookout spotted the approaching soldiers and immediately alerted his companions.

On receiving the news of the approaching army, Hall and another of the outlaws gathered up the gold and other money and carried it to a nearby cave. They divided the loot into four equal piles, stuffed each into a buckskin bag, and hastily scraped out a shallow trench in the floor of the cave into which they placed the sacks. They covered the site with rocks and debris to conceal any traces of digging. By now, Hall and his companion could hear gunshots coming from the campsite and knew that the soldiers had engaged his men in battle. Hall and his companion raced back to the camp to join in the fight.

McCullough had launched a vicious attack on the desperadoes, who were heavily outnumbered and out-armed. The fighting was brief, lasting only about five minutes. By the time it was over, three of the Union soldiers and six of the outlaws were killed. Alonzus Hall had been shot through the stomach and was in poor shape when the soldiers found him.

Hall was bandaged, loaded into a wagon, and transported to a temporary bivouac area along the White River near the present-day town of Reeds Spring, about ten miles northwest of Branson. He suffered terribly from his wound throughout the night and the next day was taken to the Union Army General Hospital at Springfield.

The attending surgeon who was summoned to treat Hall's wound was Dr. Boucher. Following an examination, Boucher deduced that a musket ball had penetrated the lower intestines, causing irreparable damage. He predicted Hall would only live another day or two.

Several hours later, Hall regained consciousness and the physician informed the outlaw of his condition. Hall appeared silent and moody, but resigned to his fate.

The next morning, however, Hall summoned Dr. Boucher to his bedside, and the outlaw asked if he could make a confession. As the surgeon was the ranking officer in the camp at the time, he agreed to take Hall's statement. Securing a hospital journal, he scribbled copious notes as Hall related the story of the recent robbery spree.

Hall told Boucher all that had transpired from the time of the Centralia Bank holdup until the attack by the Union soldiers at the campground near the White River. He said that a total of $62,000 was buried in a cave near the old ferryboat crossing where the Wilderness Road met the White River. He also asked Boucher to make certain the money he took from the farmers was returned to them.

Boucher took explicit notes of the confession, filling several pages of the journal. The next morning when he went to visit Hall, he found that the patient had died.

Boucher was confused about what to do with Hall's information. His military training told him he should immediately file it with his superiors, but the potential wealth lying buried in a shallow cave less than a day's ride from the camp tempted him greatly. With dreams of riches awaiting him, Boucher hid the journal with the expectation of someday being able to travel to the intersection of the Wilderness Road and the White River to retrieve the gold.

All too soon, however, the surgeon was transferred to a more active military post in the East. He left the journal hidden among some files at Springfield, hoping to return for it. There is no record that Dr. Boucher ever came back to Springfield. Hospital officials, during a routine examination of old files, found the old journal several years later.

By 1900 several people had read the notes made by Dr. Boucher in the journal. The descriptions of the robbery and the subsequent flight of the outlaws through the Ozark Mountains were quite vivid, as were the accounts of the encounter with the Union soldiers and the burying of the $62,000 in gold coin and other money in the shallow cave.

The journal carried a thorough description of the cave in which the gold had been cached. It was not far from an overhanging ledge a short distance from the campsite where the outlaws were attacked by the soldiers. The cavern was described as being slightly illuminated as a result of sunshine beaming through a narrow crack in the limestone roof. The men buried the loot in the cave floor at the approximate center of the shaft of light.

It is an easy task to locate the point at which the old Wilderness Road intersects with the White River—it is quite apparent on the many maps of this region. It would also seem easy to locate the overhanging ledge under which the outlaws camped, as well as any small caves in the area. An overriding problem in the search for Hall's treasure, though, is that the waters of Table Rock Lake have submerged the site!

Near where the loot is believed to have been buried, the Kimberling Bridge has been built. Some say the construction of the bridge may have obliterated any traces of the overhang and the cave. Others claim that the site is likely intact and lying under several feet of water.

There is no record or evidence that Hall's buried gold has ever been recovered. The consensus of most researchers of this event in Ozark history is that the treasure still lies in a shallow excavation in a small cave somewhere beneath the waters of Table Rock Lake.

The Ghost of Alf Bolin

Alf Bolin's reputation as a murderer and plunderer has served to make him one of several prominent outlaw legends associated with the southwestern Missouri Ozarks. Bolin's activities did not cease with his death, however, for there are many living in the region today who are convinced that his ghost still roams the countryside.

When Bolin was killed and beheaded in 1863 (see Section Four, History) Ozark residents breathed a collective sigh of relief. No longer, they believed, would they be terrorized by this badman and his cutthroat companions. Their relief was short-lived, however, for within weeks following the burial of his headless corpse in the town of Ozark, frightened citizens began reporting encounters with his ghost!

The ghost assumes two forms: One form is the head; the other is the headless body.

One night about two months following the beheading of Alf Bolin, a livery operator was walking home from his place of business, his route taking him past the courthouse where the severed head of Bolin had been mounted on a long pole and had served as a target for angry, rock-throwing citizens.

As he passed the courthouse, the liveryman heard a low moan, a sound suggesting someone was in extreme pain. Peering through the darkness, he looked toward the courthouse square from where the sound emanated, but he could see nothing. As he searched for the source of the strange noise, it came again, this time from a level about ten feet above the ground. Glancing upward, the liveryman gazed in terror at the shriveled and bloodied face of Alf Bolin hovering in the approximate spot where it had been mounted on a pole weeks earlier. Turning away from the grisly sight, the liveryman fled to his home and told his wife what he had seen.

That same night, at least three others saw the ghostly head, seemingly floating in the darkness above the courthouse square. Word of the apparition soon spread throughout the area, and nightly, dozens gathered at the edge of the square to gaze upon the ghostly head of Alf Bolin, an image that remained visible for only a few seconds at a time, moaning and screaming all the while.

Several months following the appearance of the ghost head, a second frightening form made an appearance. Near the location of Alf Bolin's burial site, a ghostly apparition was seen walking throughout the area as if looking for something. On closer inspection, the observers discovered the shadowy figure was headless! Night after night, the form appeared, and area citizens grew convinced it was Alf Bolin's headless body roaming the region in search of his severed head.

Over the years, both the head and the headless body were occasionally seen at night by hundreds of eyewitnesses until around the 1930s when the appearances grew fewer and fewer. By the 1940s, say old-timers who still live in the area, hardly anyone reported seeing the head or the body any longer.

Most of those who have seen the ghostly appearances are long gone now, and the tales of the bizarre hauntings are just a dim memory among very few. Once in a great while, though, someone walking by the old courthouse late at night will hear a low, moaning sound coming from somewhere above the ground, as if from the trees.

Alf Bolin's ghost, while not as active as it was in the past, is, according to those who claim to know, still lurking in the Ozark darkness.

Taney County's Ghost Horse

On a remote and sparsely settled stretch of unpaved road in Taney County not far from Branson, a horse is sometimes spotted behind an old, rusty, sagging barbed wire fence. Observers claim the animal appears to be searching for something or someone, pacing back and forth as it stares intently down the road. Then, suddenly and without warning, the horse will disappear, only to reappear several days later near the same spot.

A few of the residents in this southwestern Missouri county will patiently listen to outsiders' stories of encounters with this horse and then explain to them that this same horse has been seen hundreds of times—since 1925!

Taney County's population has been growing steadily since the late 1800s when immigrants from the Appalachian south began moving in. Here in this somewhat isolated portion of the Ozark Mountains, they found good water, fertile bottomlands, abundant timber, and decent graze for their livestock.

During the mid-1890s, a baby boy was born into a family of settlers who worked hard to carve out a living in the Ozarks near the town of Branson. The boy grew into an intelligent, charming, and hard-working youngster, who was admired by everyone.

The boy's prized possession was a gentle mare given to him by his father. Expertly broken to the saddle, the mare carried the boy on hundreds of rides across the fields and deep into the woods over the years. The boy cared deeply for the animal, groomed it regularly, and saw to its needs constantly. It was clear that a special relationship had developed between the boy and the horse.

In 1917 the boy, now a young man, was about to be married to a girl from a neighboring community. The two spent a great deal of time together, and, other than his mare, she seemed to be the only thing that occupied the young man's thoughts.

Weeks before the two were to be married, the United States became heavily involved in World War I. Realizing his obligation to his country, the young man enlisted into the army and was shipped to France a short time later. The marriage was postponed until such time as he returned from the war.

On November 11, 1918—seventeen months following the young man's enlistment—Armistice was declared and the soldiers were to be sent home. Celebrations were held in the tiny Ozark community in anticipation of the young man's return, and wedding plans were resumed.

A few days following the Armistice, the mare began to act strangely. While the town reveled in the good news, the horse was often seen pacing nervously in the pasture, stopping now and then to look down the road as if expecting someone.

The family related that, two days following the Armistice, the mare broke through the pasture fence and, when the family awoke the next morning, was found standing outside her master's bedroom window.

The gentle, easygoing mare had never behaved in this manner in the past, and the family attributed it to advanced age. That afternoon, the fence was repaired and the mare was led back to the pasture.

The next evening, however, she broke out again and returned to the same place just outside the window. This time, she knocked the screen out and pushed her head into the room. When the young man's mother entered the room, she saw the horse frantically searching about the interior. At that point, the family began to believe something terrible had happened to the young man.

Two days later, the family received a telegram stating that the young man had been killed in one of the final battles of the war only hours before the Armistice was signed.

The mare lived on for another seven years and finally died quietly in the pasture. Several months following the death of the mare, a passer-by reported seeing it standing against the fence near the road. When he told the young man's family, they assumed he was just mistaken, that it must have been another horse. As weeks passed, however, others reported seeing the mare positioned near the road behind the fence, staring into the distance as if in anticipation of someone's arrival.

As the years passed, towns like Branson and Springfield grew in population, and more and more people left the small rural countryside and moved into the cities. Many of the small communities and farms were simply abandoned and left to ruin.

Tourists often drive along the old roads that once linked some of those early communities. They revel in the autumn foliage and the picturesque Ozark countryside, and they stop now and then to inspect or photograph an old log barn or rustic homeplace.

And once in a while, someone will comment on spotting a single mare while driving along a remote, long-unused pasture. The mare, oblivious to travelers, looks fixedly down the lonely road as if expecting someone special to arrive.

The traveler may glance away for a second, but when he looks back, the mare is gone!

The Little People

Monsters can come in a variety of sizes. The remote environs of portions of the southwestern Missouri Ozarks are reputedly the home of a tribe of monsters that grow to a height of less than two-and-a-half feet tall! In spite of their size, they have been responsible, according to legend and lore, for a number of killings and for terrorizing that portion of the Ozarks that overlaps their domain.

The folklore of several dozen Indian tribes contains references to what are generally referred to as the "little people." For some tribes, the little people are regarded as spirits that inspire and perform positive acts. Other tribes consider the little people demons with an apparent propensity for evil.

Stories attributed to the Osage Indians occasionally mention the little people who lived in the Ozark Mountains in Stone and Taney Counties. Long before the settlement of whites in this area, the Indians who frequented the region were forced to contend with the depredations of the vicious, malicious little people.

Described as being no more than two-and-a-half feet tall, these strange Ozark little people possessed a dark brown skin similar to the color and texture of tanned leather. Covered in a fine brown fur, they went about totally naked and traveled in bands of no more than six or seven. In addition to their diminutive stature, the most remarkable features of the little people were their fierce visages and their disproportionately long and razor sharp teeth. Their misshapen heads contained cruel, glaring eyes that seemed far too large. Their movements were quick, almost squirrel-like, and they were capable of running through the woods at a high rate of speed. It was said that a group of them could bring down a deer and kill it within mere seconds.

The little people often attacked the hunting camps of the Indians who frequented the area. One story relates an incident where a hunting party departed camp, leaving one of its members to watch over the horses. When the hunters returned the next day, their companion, as well as one of the horses, had been killed and partially eaten by the little people. Before he fell to their attack, the Indian had killed one of the tiny monsters, and the curious little body was carried from village to village for several years.

References to the little people were also found in the journals of French explorers who entered this area. Time and again, exploration and trapping parties were forced to fight off nightly attacks by the hideous little folk.

Early white settlers in this area reported a number of encounters with the little people. After losing livestock and even an occasional citizen to the fierce, carnivorous creatures, armed parties of settlers entered the woods and hunted them down, often killing as many as three or four in a single night. After several months of these nightly hunts, depredations slowed and eventually ceased altogether.

To this day, however, backpackers who spend the night in the Ozark woods of southwestern Missouri sometimes report strange visitations by small forms they describe as human-like in appearance with oversize eyes and grotesque heads.

Some Interesting Places and Place Names

The Ozark Mountains have long fascinated visitors for a number of reasons, and one of them has to do with the numerous and colorful place names found throughout the region, many of them close to Branson.

The formal study of place names is called toponymy. The names people give to places—settlements, streams, hills, knobs, valleys—can reveal much about the local culture and cultural origins, and sometimes serve as a method to determine where the initial settlers came from and what their influences may have been.

The Ozarks are rich in interesting and culturally distinct toponyms. In Missouri, one can find places such as Ink, Rat, Impo, Bucksnort Creek, Black Jack, Bourbon, Cabool, Tightwad, Needmore, Shakerag, Peculiar, Racket, and Monkey Run. Arkansas offers Fifty-Six, Ben Hur, Pickles Gap, Skunk Hollow, Toad Suck, Congo, and Clyde.

Near Branson, a number of toponyms are associated with animals: Bear Creek, Bee Creek, Bull Creek, Coon Creek, Doe Hollow, Mutton Hollow, Turkey Creek, and Wildcat Hollow. Some names for features have been derived from area vegetation, such as Willow Springs and

Oak Hill. Other names are derived from occupations—Limekiln Hollow and Sawmill Hollow. Below are some interesting places and place names, all within a short drive from Branson.

Aunts Creek

Aunts Creek campsite is located on Table Rock Lake just a few short miles west of Branson. Local old-timers claim the site was named after an early resident, but they have long since forgotten whom.

Aurora

Aurora, thirty miles northwest of Branson, was the center of the region's lead and zinc mining boom between 1887 and 1920. When the ores were mined out, the town reverted to being a service center for area farms. The largest employer here is the Juvenile Shoe Corporation.

Buffalo

The town of Buffalo, a one-hour drive north of Branson, is a reminder of the times when a species of bison called the forest buffalo used to roam this area. The *Buffalo Reflex* is the name of the town's newspaper.

Carthage

Located about seventy miles northwest of Branson, the town of Carthage was once burned down by Confederate soldiers during the Civil War. In spite of the destruction, Carthage recovered nicely during the lead-mining and marble-quarrying era that followed and today is a thriving city.

Cassville

A town of approximately 2,000 residents in nearby Barry County, Cassville generally serves as a center for businesses related to the area farms and settlements. The town, named after an early settler, once served as the capital for the Confederate members of the Missouri General Assembly.

Cow Creek

Cow Creek is a tributary of the White River that feeds into Table Rock Lake and was named after the herds of livestock that commonly grazed in the area before the development of tourism.

Dewey Bald

A bald is a bare expanse of rock elevated somewhat above the surrounding terrain. Dewey Bald, a prominent feature seen from Table Rock Lake, is featured in Harold Bell Wright's book *The Shepherd of the Hills*.

Diamond

Diamond is noted for being the home of the famous black educator and agricultural scientist George Washington Carver. Originally named Diamond Grove Prairie, this interesting little town is located about sixty miles northwest of Branson.

Eagle Rock

Another Table Rock location, this site was named after the American eagle, once a common resident of the area often seen snatching up fish from the surface of the lake years earlier.

Eureka Springs

This Carroll County, Arkansas, town is located some thirty-five miles southwest of Branson. The springs that gush out of the limestone rock were long known to the Indians who frequented the area, and were later used by early white settlers. In fact, Eureka Springs' initial growth was due to the perceived healing power of the springs. Today, Eureka Springs is a major tourist destination in northwestern Arkansas and features shopping, music, and fine restaurants.

Forsyth

Forsyth is located a few miles east of Branson and is currently a farm and recreational service center. The vigilante organization the Bald Knobbers (see Section Four, History of the Branson Area) was founded on a nearby bald.

Galena

The county seat of Stone County, Missouri, Galena was named after the bluish-gray mineral considered to be the principal ore of lead, which was mined nearby at one time. One of the smallest county seats in Missouri, Galena boasts a population of less than five hundred.

Ginger Blue

This town with the unique name is located on the Elk River and is one of the Ozarks' oldest and most popular fishing camps. The restaurant at the resort is known nationwide for its fine cuisine.

Granby

Granby is the oldest lead and zinc mining town in the Ozark Mountains. When lead was discovered here during the 1950s, the town grew rapidly only to dwindle when the ore was eventually depleted.

Horseshoe Bend

Horseshoe Bend is located eight miles east of Rogers, Arkansas, on Highway 94. The site was named as a result of the pronounced bend in the river at this point that resembles a horseshoe.

Joe Bald

Joe Bald is located a short distance from Branson. According to researchers, no one living in the area today knows who the "Joe" was after whom this bald was named.

Lead Hill

Located in Boone County, Arkansas, approximately twenty-five miles southeast of Branson, Lead Hill was named after the discovery and mining of lead that occurred in the region decades ago.

Murder Rocks

Located a short distance east of Branson, the Murder Rocks are composed of sandstone weathered into curiously formed pinnacles standing approximately fifteen feet high. During the Civil War, outlaws used the Murder Rocks as a hiding place. From this location, they were known to attack and kill travelers on the nearby road.

Mutton Hollow

Located just west of Branson, Mutton Hollow was the site of early settlement in this region and was named after the herds of sheep that grazed here.

Neosho

Located sixty miles west of Branson, Neosho is likely most famous for being the home of the noted American painter Thomas Hart Benton.

Nogo

Now a ghost town located just east of Springfield, Nogo was once a substantial community with a school. When the community first grew large enough to support a railroad station, the residents petitioned to name it Orchard Hill. The railroad, however, would not accept the name. A meeting was held, and one man, speaking of the rejection of the name Orchard Hill, said it was "No go." Someone at the meeting spoke up and said to just name the town Nogo. And they did!

Oronogo

This small community of just over five hundred residents is located northwest of Branson in Jasper County. Once a center for lead and zinc mining, Oronogo is filled with abandoned buildings and houses reminiscent of a more successful time.

This interesting town had several names—Leadville Hollow, Center Creek, and Minersville—before becoming Oronogo. During a town meeting held to change the name of Minersville to something else, a man committed to associating the community with the mining activity stated, "By God, boys, it's ore or no go!" Another voiced the opinion that the town should then be named Oronogo, and it was.

Panther Bay

Located ten miles east of Mountain Home, Arkansas, on Norfork Lake, Panther Bay was named after the animal that frequented this region in great numbers over one hundred years ago. Other names for panther include cougar, mountain lion, painter, and catamount.

Pomme de Terre

A French name, Pomme de Terre literally means "fruit of the earth." Pomme de Terre Lake and State Park is located just west of Highway 65, approximately a one-hour drive north of Branson. The lake, a favorite place for area residents during the summer, is known for good fishing, and the park offers a boat ramp, boat rentals, picnicking, and camping opportunities.

Ponce de Leon

The tiny community of Ponce de Leon was named after the Spanish explorer who allegedly searched for the Fountain of Youth. The name was selected because of the number of free flowing springs found in the area.

Reeds Spring

Reeds Spring, population just under five hundred, is a neighbor to Branson, located a few miles to the northwest on Table Rock Lake. A picturesque and friendly little town, Reeds Spring often receives travelers and tourists who enjoy shopping along the canopied sidewalks.

Rockaway Beach

Rockaway Beach, named after a resort location in New York, was initially known as Taneycomo. Originally founded by early residents Willard and Anna Merriam, Rockaway Beach was a setting for some of the earliest successful musical performances in the Branson area. Today, it is considered to be mostly a trout fishing resort.

Seneca

Seneca lies adjacent to the only tripoli deposit ever considered commercially important in the United States. This soft and fibrous silica is often in high demand as a filter for municipal water systems and as an important filler compound for rubber.

Seymour

Seymour is located on U.S. Highway 60 just a few miles east of Springfield. Once a major apple-growing center for this part of the Ozarks, Seymour is now home to several Amish families who originally migrated to the area from Indiana during the 1950s and 1960s.

Splitlog

This southwestern Missouri community was named after a Wyandotte Indian known as Matthias Splitlog. Originally the town was built around the prospect of mining silver in the area, but when no ore was ever located, the citizens abandoned it. Today, Splitlog is considered a ghost town.

Sulphur Springs

Sulphur Springs, located in the far northwestern tip of Arkansas, was named after the sulphur-laden spring waters that were once popular. During the late 1800s and early 1900s, visitors from Arkansas, Missouri, Oklahoma, even from as far away as Iowa and Minnesota, would come to the springs to soak in the presumed-to-be healing waters.

Taneycomo

A composite of the words Taney, county, and Missouri, Lake Taneycomo is the long, sinuous body of water that flows through a portion of Branson. The present-day town of Rockaway Beach was once known as Taneycomo.

Three Johns School District

As a result of a great deal of bickering and ill feelings relative to choosing a name for a Taney County school district, the issue was finally settled when it was named Three Johns, after the first names of three members of the school board. A rumor that circulated around the county for a time during the 1970s led people to believe the district was a reference to three bathrooms!

Tontitown

Tontitown, named after the Italian explorer Henri de Tonti, is located just west of Springdale, Arkansas, and about sixty miles southwest of Branson. The town was originally settled by Italian immigrants who fled from their earlier homes in the malaria-infested environs of southeastern Arkansas. At Tontitown, they grew grapes and established several wineries along with a grape juice cannery. Each year, the Tontitown Grape Festival attracts visitors from several states.

Verona

Verona was once considered the largest strawberry-producing area in the Missouri Ozarks. During the 1870s, a group of Waldensians made their home nearby. The Waldensians were a Protestant Separatist group from Italy who arrived here by way of South America!

Branson: America's New Music and Entertainment Capital!

Theaters and Music Halls

It has been observed by writers, critics, and fans that Branson has more live entertainment at any given time of the day than any other city in America. Country and western, bluegrass, gospel, pop, western, rock and roll, classical, jazz, and Broadway-style music ring from the numerous theaters and music halls found throughout the environs. Branson is home to almost forty concert theaters, ranging in seating from 400 to 4,000, and each theater offers between one and four shows daily. What is even more phenomenal is that most of the performances play to capacity audiences.

Music has a long and successful history in Branson. In 1959 the Baldknobbers Jamboree opened to delighted visitors, offering performances of mountain music, gospel music, and comedy. As time went by, and as word-of-mouth descriptions of the entertainment goings-on in Branson filtered across much of the United States, more and more visitors began arriving in the region to participate in the fun.

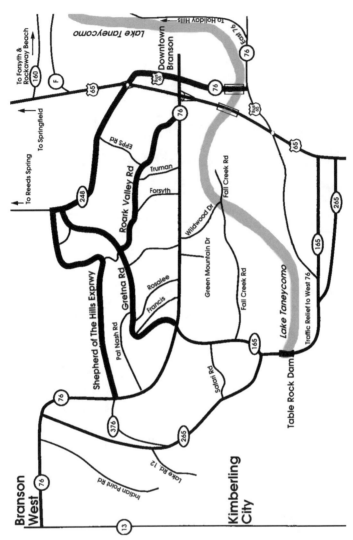

Branson, Missouri. The entertainment strip (Highway 76) is located west of Highway 65. Historic downtown Branson is located east of the highway.

The "Strip," Branson, Missouri!

Impressed with the huge crowds and the extremely positive audience response, some established country and western performers began migrating to Branson and opening up showplaces of their own. Among the first "name" C&W showmen to arrive were Roy Clark and Mel Tillis. Soon, they were followed by a host of others who have chosen to live out their careers in the entertainment mecca Branson has come to be.

As the country and western showplaces grew in popularity, and as Branson was clearly becoming an important and favored tourist destination, representatives from other musical styles including Broadway, bluegrass, gospel, patriotic, and rock and roll found a home here.

Music of all kinds, along with humor and dancing, can be found aplenty in this small southwestern Missouri town. Performances tend to be relaxed and friendly, and the entertainers often visit with members of the audience and sign autographs after the shows.

One is seldom without an opportunity to attend a musical performance in Branson. Shows begin at the breakfast hour and continue throughout the day and well into the night. Many visitors see three or four shows a day. A great many of the shows are family oriented and offer wholesome entertainment for all. Many of the shows, in fact, are performed by families, including the Baldknobbers, the Presleys, the Osmond Brothers, the Lennon Sisters, and the Lennon Brothers. In addition, stars such as Tony Orlando, Bobby Vinton, and Shoji Tabuchi include members of their immediate families in the performances.

Although Branson and the southwestern Missouri Ozark Mountains attract visitors from across the country and overseas for a variety of excellent reasons, this special region has become most closely associated with music than anything else.

Ticket prices for most of Branson's shows change from year to year. The visitor is advised to obtain a show schedule on arriving. If you care to plan ahead, write to the Branson/Lakes Area Chamber of Commerce for the most up-to-date listings of concerts and shows. The chamber will also put the prospective visitor in touch with ticket and travel agents.

Americana Theater
2905 76 Country Boulevard

Called the Most Recognized Show in Branson, Jennifer appears at the Americana Theater both in the morning and in the evening. One of the most popular shows in Branson, Jennifer, a one-time USO performer, combines her many talents—singing, dancing, comedy— in this fast-paced family-oriented show with her great band, The Prime Time Pickers.

Costumes, dancing, singing, and comedy highlight these spirited performances. Jennifer was voted Entertainer of the Year by the AAMA in 1994, 1995, 1996.

Jennifer's Americana Theater

Children get in free at the Americana Theater. For more information or to make reservations call (417) 33-JENNIFER.

Baldknobbers Hillbilly Jamboree Show
2825 76 Country Boulevard

They started it all!

The first musical show in Branson, the Baldknobbers have played continuously since 1959 and feature country hits and classics as well as ragtime piano and comedy.

The Baldknobbers got their start during the 1950s on a Springfield radio station. The four Mabe brothers—Bill, Jim, Lyle, and Bob—were the original members. To this day, the Mabes, a longtime Ozark family, make up the nucleus of the Baldknobbers.

The evening show is a high-energy, delightfully corny performance filled with jokes, costumes, hillbillyana, and, of course, some fine music performed by talented musicians and singers. The program begins in the evening and lasts well into the night. Everyone gets his or her money's worth here!

The Baldknobbers Jamboree Show

The Baldknobbers Hillbilly Jamboree Show is open from March to mid-December, and the associated restaurant serves up fine food.

BoxCar Willie Theater
3454 76 Country Boulevard

BoxCar Willie, whose real name is Leland Travis Martin, was one of Branson's first commercially successful performers. Box, as his friends call him, is backed by his own band, The Texas Trainmen, and performs classic country songs about hobos, trains, and the open road.

Occasional guests at the BoxCar Willie Theater include Ferlin Huskey and Ronnie Prophet. Huskey, famous for his 1950s hit song "Gone," has enjoyed a country and pop music career over a period spanning five decades.

Ronnie Prophet, a veteran country music performer, has won awards for CCMA Entertainer of the Year, Country Male Vocalist of the Year, Television Country Show of the Year, and Outstanding Performance by a Male Country Singer. His two-hour family-oriented show is filled with music and comedy.

Ferlin Husky is best remembered for his longtime number one song "Wings of a Dove," the number five most popular song of all time! His breakfast show includes many of his fine hits as well as his alter-ego Simon Crum.

The 900-seat BoxCar Willie Theater is open April through December. The BoxCar Willie Museum, located next door to the theater, is well worth a visit.

The BoxCar Willie showplace

Branson Mall Music Theater
2200 76 Country Boulevard

This 500-seat theater is located next to Branson's Wal-Mart! The featured attraction at the Branson Mall Theater is Bob Nichols, who performs country music, swing, rock and roll, bluegrass, and gospel. Nichols is noted for rendering some of the most spirited yodeling heard in the Ozarks.

Award-winning Johnny Lee also performs at the Branson Mall Music Theater. Lee, who appeared in the hit movie *Urban Cowboy*, has had fourteen number one hits, including "Lookin' for Love in All the Wrong Places," "Cherokee Fiddle," "Pickin' Up Strangers," and "Yellow Rose of Texas."

Open all year long, the Branson Mall Music Theater occasionally features guest stars such as: The Ragin' Cajun Doug Kershaw and his amazing fiddle playing; Italian crooner Peter Lemongello, who performs at the morning show (9:30 A.M.); and Allen Edwards, who comes on at 12:15 to delight the lunch crowd.

Branson Showcase America Theater
Missouri Highway 248 and U.S. 65

Housed in the former Glen Campbell Goodtime Theater, the new Branson Showcase America Theater will feature a variety of nationally prominent musical and comedy entertainers. This 2,240-seat theater will offer everything from gospel music to the Beach Boys to Crytal Gayle to Blood, Sweat, and Tears. There will be different performers every day and shows three times a day.

Branson Stage Theater
3600 76 Country Boulevard

Branson Stage Theater is noted for featuring family-oriented entertainment. The award-winning Hughes

Brothers quartet gets things started early with a singing and dancing morning show at 10:00 A.M.

At 2:30 P.M. Ragtime Lil and Banjo-Banjo present a Dixieland Show reminiscent of the Roaring Twenties.

In the evening, Sagebrush, a Broadway-style musical of the Old West offers spirited entertainment and colorful western costumes.

Braschler Music Show Theater
3044 Shepherd of the Hills Expressway

One of the original Branson family music shows, the Braschlers feature country tunes and plenty of comedy. Considered to be one of the most enduring groups in the Ozarks, the Braschlers opened their theater in 1986. Playing to capacity crowds, this show has gained a reputation as one of the most popular gospel acts in the area.

Recent guests at the Braschler Music Show Theater have included noted western song stylists Sons of the Pioneers, who perform regularly. The Sons of the Pioneers sang backup harmonies for Roy Rogers throughout much of the 1930s and 1940s.

The Braschler Music Show Theater is open April through December.

Anita Bryant Theater
3446 76 Country Boulevard

Former singing star, Miss Oklahoma (1958), and one-time spokesperson for the Florida orange juice producers Anita Bryant has built one of the most successful theaters in Branson. After recording thirty record albums and authoring ten books, this one-time USO entertainer dedicates much of her show toward paying tribute to Armed Forces veterans. Her performances contain many of her famous hit records, such as "Paper Roses" and "My Little Corner of the World," along with other 1950s tunes and several gospel numbers.

The Anita Bryant Theater is open February through December.

Roy Clark Celebrity Theater
3425 76 Country Boulevard

Roy Clark was the first "name" Nashville performer to settle in Branson. Impressed with the audience reaction of the Baldknobbers and the Presleys, Clark constructed his theater and began spending more and more of his time here. The former host of television's popular *Hee Haw*, Clark is called the Czar of Guitar, and he continues to dazzle audiences with his award-winning guitar artistry. Clark has delighted country music fans for over three decades, and critics claim his Branson show is the best ever.

Guest stars at the Roy Clark Celebrity Theater include Doug Gabriel, regarded as one of Branson's most popular singers, who presents a high-energy show mornings and evenings.

The Roy Clark Celebrity Theater

Country Tonight Theater
4080 76 Country Boulevard

Awarded the Best Live Country Show in America in 1994, 1995, and 1996, this performance features wholesome family entertainment with lively country music, square dancing, line dancing, fiddling, and clogging, all laced through and through with comedy. Country Tonight Theater also claims the number one fiddler of the year as well as the number one dance group in Branson!

Though the theater features few nationally prominent headline acts, most of the performers who play here are top-flight musicians from Las Vegas and Nashville. Many of the performers, in fact, are children as young as ten years of age!

These young and extremely talented performers offer a high-energy act that leaves patrons breathless. Enjoy everything from old Roy Rogers tunes to rocking country music to rope tricks to the world champion yodeler!

The morning show at the Country Tonight Theater features Golden Girls USA, a sentimental salute to Armed Forces veterans.

The Country Tonight Theater is open March through December.

Dixie Stampede
1527 76 Country Boulevard

One of the newest entries in the Branson theater sweepstakes, the Dixie Stampede is the brainchild of award-winning singer, songwriter, and television and movie star Dolly Parton. Paired with a restaurant, this 110,000-square-foot dinner theater offers singing, dancing, and dazzling costumes in a Civil War setting.

The Dixie Stampede is open March through December.

Dolly Parton's Dixie Stampede

Dogwood Theater
1420 76 Country Boulevard

This new theater located in the Dogwood Inn features The Texans Quartet Music Show. The Texans feature fun for the entire family with country and gospel music sprinkled with selections of oldies and comedy. The Texans have been named Texas Gospel Group of the Year seven times!

Also featured at the Dogwood Theater are vocalist Cindi Barr and Boy Howdy, well-known Branson comedian. For more information call (417) 334-2321.

Barbara Fairchild Theater
3115 76 Country Boulevard

Barbara Fairchild, the personable, longtime popular country singer and two-time Grammy Award nominee, has built an entertaining show around country and gospel music and teddy bears! (Her biggest hit was called "Teddy Bear.") You have to see it to believe it.

On Sundays, Fairchild hosts a free two-hour worship service and music program. Come early, because this show is normally packed.

The Barbara Fairchild Theater is open April through December.

The Barbara Fairchild Theater

'50s Variety Theater
3105 76 Country Boulevard

The "At The Hop Show" offers a hearty dose of 1950s rock and roll music and nostalgia featuring the songs of Elvis Presley, Buddy Holly, Roy Orbison, and the Everly Brothers. Lively, action-packed dance numbers, crisp singing, and a touch of comedy make this one of Branson's most popular shows.

Special guests at the '50s Variety Theater in the past have included Peter Lemongello, billed as Branson's Italian Crooner. Lemongello has been a frequent guest on

The Tonight Show, Merv Griffin, Dinah Shore, and Mike Douglas.

The '50s Variety Theater is open mid-March through late December.

Mickey Gilley Theater
3455 West Highway 76

The principal attraction at the Mickey Gilley Theater is Gilley himself, performing his numerous country hits and featuring his impressive piano artistry. Gilley's repertoire ranges from warm ballads to up-tempo rockers. Backed up by the Urban Cowboy Band, Gilley, a cousin to both rocker Jerry Lee Lewis and evangelist Jimmy Swaggart, has been a major country artist for two decades. Gilley is the former owner of Gilleys, the Houston country and western music palace that has been dubbed the "world's largest honky tonk." In his amazing career, he has had 39 top ten hits and 17 number one songs! The Branson version of Gilley's is a comfortable 950-seat theater.

After touring and performing for twenty-five years, Gilley decided to settle in Branson and perform at his own showplace.

Moe Bandy, a regular performer at the Mickey Gilley Theater, is also an established country music performer and has been recording and singing for over twenty years. He sings his hits "It's a Cheating Situation" and "Till I'm Too Old to Die Young." His Gilley's show features his greatest hits as well as gospel, patriotic, and a return to his Texas roots in his Rodeo Review. Bandy also does some excellent impersonations of popular singers and has a finely honed comedic routine. Bandy's comedy partner is the noted songwriter and comedian Don Bowman.

Jim Owen, a well-known writer and performer, is another regular guest of Gilley's Theater. This Emmy Award-winning performer and star of two Hank Williams movies sings Hank Williams songs the way Hank sang them decades ago.

Former Grand Ol' Opry announcer Bill Cole said Jim Owen presents "my favorite show...ever...!"

The Mickey Gilley Theater is open March through December. For information and reservations call (417) 334-3210.

The Mickey Gilley Theater

Grand Palace
2700 76 Country Boulevard

The Springfield *News Leader* called the Grand Palace the "Carnegie Hall of Branson."

During the course of the entertainment season, many of the nation's leading country music stars are booked into the Grand Palace, Branson's largest theater. This magnificent structure holds 4,000 people and was constructed at a cost of $13 million. The original developers who gave rise to the theater included Silver Dollar City and country music star Kenny Rogers. Rogers eventually divorced himself from the operation in 1995, and one year later Silver Dollar City pulled out and went on to other projects. The Grand Palace Theater, however, remains Branson's premier showplace.

The Grand Palace is a treat to the eye, featuring antebellum architecture, expensive chandeliers, and other gorgeous trappings.

The great Barbara Mandrell is a regular performer at the Grand Palace. Called one of the most energetic entertainers in this entertainment capital of America's Heartland, Mandrell sings her award-winning songs, dances, and plays several instruments.

In addition to the popular performers who appear here, the regular headliner at the Grand Palace is performer Dino, an acclaimed pianist. Dino presents the spectacular show "Music For All Time," a million-dollar production featuring lavish sets, stunning costumes, elaborate full stage dance routines, a dazzling light show, and the vocals of his lovely wife, Cheryl.

The Grand Palace

Reta Lee's Country Music Club
3559 Shepherd of the Hills Expressway

Reta Lee, a former Las Vegas singer and dancer, offers a lively and exciting luncheon and dinner show.

Also appearing is comedian Elmer Fudpucker, whose humor has delighted audiences from coast to coast for over a decade.

Mutton Hollow Entertainment Park

Mutton Hollow Entertainment Park offers a wide variety of entertainment throughout the year, occasionally featuring stars such as The Platters, the premier 1950s group that had great hits such as "The Great Pretender" and "Only You." (For location and times, see Section Eight, Theme Parks.)

Wayne Newton Theater
3701 76 Country Boulevard

What eventually became the Wayne Newton Theater has an odd history. It began as a concept called Cash Country, and was originally planned as a showplace for country and western superstars June Carter and Johnny Cash. It never materialized, however, and eventually opened as the Five Star Theater, featuring an orangutan act and magic show. In the meantime, a smaller theater was being constructed across town for Las Vegas showman and singer Wayne Newton. Ultimately, the orangutan act left town, the magician moved into the original Wayne Newton building, and Newton himself moved into the larger structure, which was renamed, logically, the Wayne Newton Theater. Newton performed here for one year and returned to Las Vegas. In 1997 Newton returned to Branson to perform at the Tony Orlando Yellow Ribbon Theater in between Orlando's engagements.

The current Wayne Newton Theater is expected to undergo a name change and an entirely new slate of acts will be booked, so for more information call on arriving.

Tony Orlando Yellow Ribbon Theater
3220 Falls Parkway at Highway 165

Best known for his international 1970s hits "Tie a Yellow Ribbon 'Round the Old Oak Tree," "Knock Three Times," and "Candida," Orlando delights packed houses with sing-alongs and greatest hit performances. This personable showman, who has considerable television and Las Vegas experience, interacts constantly with the audience members, alternately charming them and getting them to sing along. It works, for folks return time after time for these great performances.

One of the most popular showplaces in Branson, the Tony Orlando Yellow Ribbon Theater is open March through late December.

Osmond Family Theater
3216 76 Country Boulevard

The Osmond Family Theater features the family that gained national fame on the Lawrence Welk Show. In addition to the brothers, the Osmond Family Theater also features the Osmond Second Generation, figure skaters The Ice Angels, the juggling artistry of T.J. Howell, the magic of the Hammers, and Bob Moore and his Amazing Mongrels.

The range of the Osmond performances, which have been going on since 1992, never ceases to amaze capacity audiences as the brothers move easily from barbershop quartet numbers to country music to pop and classic renditions of favorite tunes.

Not to be missed at the Osmond's Family Theater is John Stuart's world famous Legends In Concert. Legends In Concert is a live, on-stage recreation of the performances of legendary superstars of the past and present, including Elvis, Marilyn Monroe, Neil Diamond, Tom Jones, Elton John, The Blues Brothers, Liberace, Roy Orbison, Tina Turner, and many, many more.

Legends In Concert also features state-of-the-art lighting and a host of incredibly talented singers and dancers.

The Osmond Family Theater is open March through December.

For information and reservations call (417) 336-6100.

The Osmond Family Theater

Owens Theater
205 South Commercial Street

Master entertainer Dave Ehlert skillfully offers impersonations of Elvis Presley, Tom Jones, Liberace, Johnny Mathis, Neil Diamond, Ray Charles, Roy Orbison, Willie Nelson, and Wolfman Jack. Ehlert, incidentally, was the first person ever inducted into the Elvis Impersonators Worldwide Hall of Fame!

The Owens Theater is open all year.

Presleys' Jubilee Theater
2920 76 Country Boulevard

Presleys' was Branson's first music show and today is called a Branson landmark! Over the years the costumes have changed, the acts have become more polished, and a host of talented performers have been added, but the show at Presleys', featuring three generations of the family, still maintains the original spark that has entertained millions of visitors.

Country, as well as gospel music, along with a healthy dose of humor and antics, have made Presleys' one of the most popular shows in Branson. Publications such as *Country Weekly* and *Country America Yearbook* have praised the Presleys' show as one of the best in the country.

Presleys' Jubilee

The theater is open March through December. Plan well ahead of time to attend the Presleys' Jubilee Theater, since this extremely popular show is usually sold out early.

For information and reservations call (417) 334-4874.

Charley Pride Theater
Gretna Road at Wildwood Drive

Charley Pride has become something of a legend during his thirty-plus years as a country and western performer. The first commercially successful black C & W performer, Pride has sold over 30 million records, had 35 number one hits, and won three Grammys. Next to Elvis

Presley, Pride, according to his biography, has sold more records for RCA than anyone else!

Pride took the country music scene by storm back during the 1960s and 1970s with such giant hits as "Is Anybody Going to San Antone" and "Kiss an Angel Good Morning." Still active as a performer and in the recording studio, Pride has now made Branson his permanent home.

Regular guests at the Charley Pride Theater include the Oak Ridge Boys and the Janie Fricke and Jimmy Travis Show.

The Oak Ridge Boys have generated an incredible number of hits during the past twenty years. Four-part harmonies, dynamic showmanship, and heart-pounding, foot-stomping rhythms make the Oaks one of the country's most sought-after acts. The Oaks began as a gospel quartet, but a change in personnel and musical philosophy led to the crossover hit "The Y'all Come Back Saloon." Since then, they have remained on top of the country music charts with dozens of country and pop hits and have won accolades ranging from Grammys to Country Music Association Awards.

The Janie Fricke and Jimmy Travis Show is a treat for all ages. Fricke, once one of the most sought-after harmony singers for Nashville recording sessions, is a three-time winner of the prestigious Female Vocalist of the Year Award. Travis provides impressive musicianship for this entertaining act.

Jerry Reed—singer, musician, humorist, and movie actor—has had an incredible string of hit songs including "Amos Moses" and "When You're Hot You're Hot." Reed's show is a continuous hand-clapping, knee-slapping good time enjoyed by adults and children alike.

The Charley Pride Theater seats 1,974 and is open April through December.

For information and reservations call (417) 33-PRIDE.

Pump Boys and Dinettes Dinner Theater
P.O. Box 8028

This attractive dinner theater presents the popular and award-winning musical comedy production set in an old-time gas station and diner.

This ninety-one-minute, Tony-nominated show is packed with twenty-one songs. The humorous script, along with the excellent actors and talented musicians, blends nicely in this fun-filled musical tribute to life's simple pleasures.

The menu at the Pump Boys and Dinettes Dinner Theater includes prime rib, baked chicken, baked fish, BBQ ribs, and meatloaf. The theater is also open for lunch, serving fine food as well as great entertainment.

Broadway for Breakfast is featured in the morning at the theater and includes a musical revue of some of the best loved songs from Broadway musicals.

The musical is performed during the entire year. From January to April it is limited to the dinner performance. The lunch show begins in April.

Will Rogers Theater
U.S. Highway 65 at Highway 248

The well-received performance of *Promise*, an epic religious musical drama, is the current and probably ongoing feature at the Will Rogers Theater.

Promise has been performed around the world, including Russia and Europe, and has been seen by millions. Spectacular stage settings, colorful costumes, special effects, and a cast of over fifty performers take this show to impressive entertainment and inspirational heights.

This epic musical based on the life of Jesus Christ is one of the most popular shows in Branson, with visitors returning time and again to watch the stunning performance.

Promise is performed April through December. For reservations and information call (417) 336-1333 or 1-800-687-4752.

76 Music Hall
1945 76 Country Boulevard

This 556-seat theater offers four different shows each day throughout the week.

The Brumley Music Show had its beginning with Albert E. Brumley Sr., who wrote over eight hundred folk and gospel classics including the popular standards "I'll Fly Away," "Turn Your Radio On," and "Jesus Hold My Hand."

Today's version of the Brumleys is a third-generation family show featuring steel guitarist Tom Brumley, who was once voted the country's number one steel guitarist by the Association of County Music. Brumley has performed with Buck Owens and the Buckaroos, Rick Nelson and the Stone Canyon Band, and the Desert Rose Band. Brumley has also worked on recording sessions with many of the top names in country music.

The Downhome Country Music Show offers country music and western swing. The skilled musicians and performers are lead by Splinter Middleton, noted for his impersonations of Johnny Cash, George Jones, Hank Williams, and Willie Nelson.

The Texas Gold Miners' enthusiasm is catching as they serve up toe-tapping music, clogging, and comedy.

76 Country USA is an action-packed, upbeat country show featuring quartet harmonies, comedy, gospel, and a patriotic finish.

76 Music Hall

Sunday Gospel Jubilee provides old-time gospel music from the Bacon Family on Sunday afternoons while the Ozark Mountain Jubilee provides Sunday morning entertainment.

The 76 Music Hall is open all year long.

Silver Dollar City
Indian Point Road

This popular theme park features over fifty spectacular stage shows daily—singing and dancing with a cast of hundreds. Silver Dollar City also hosts the Great American Music Festival during May and June, a celebration of bluegrass, gospel, jazz, and more with 100 shows daily.

Silver Dollar City is open mid-April through December (see Theme Parks, Section Eight).

Jim Stafford Theater
3440 76 Country Boulevard

Family-oriented entertainment is the thrust of the Jim Stafford Theater, and he features a variety of special effects, nonstop comedy, and great music.

Stafford, known for his hits "Spiders and Snakes" and "Cow Patti," as well as a short-lived television show, serves up healthy portions of comedy and music along with flying saucers, dancing chickens, stampeding cows, and marching bands. Wild and fun-filled, Stafford's shows leave audiences alternately spellbound and rolling with laughter. The Stafford show is action packed and especially enjoyable for children.

It is obvious from watching a Jim Stafford performance that this entertainer truly loves what he is doing. Among Branson residents and other performers, Stafford remains a favorite.

The Jim Stafford Theater

Try world-acclaimed banjoist Buck Trent for a country music morning at the Jim Stafford Theater. Trent, former star of television's *Hee Haw* and a two-time Country Music Association Instrumentalist of the Year, is accompanied by Mary Lou Turner and Kenney Parrot to bring music and fun to breakfasters.

Shoji Tabuchi Theater
3260 Shepherd of the Hills Expressway

Many consider Shoji Tabuchi the best fiddle player in the world. A violin player by the age of seven, Tabuchi was inspired by a Roy Acuff concert in his home of Osaka, Japan, as a teenager, and determined to learn how to play the country and bluegrass style of fiddle. Tabuchi's incredible repertoire ranges from bluegrass to classical, Cajun to swing, Broadway show tunes to country. Furthermore, he fiddles upside down and backwards. Backed by an eighteen-piece orchestra, this incredible fiddle act is accompanied by a laser light show and other special effects that leave the audience gasping.

The Shoji Tabuchi Theater opened in 1990 and is regarded today as one of the most ornately decorated and lighted theaters in America, both inside and out.

The Shoji Tabuchi Theater is open March through December.

The Thunderbird Theater
2215 76 Country Boulevard

This 700-seat theater is noted primarily for the Blackwood Family morning show, a powerful gospel program augmented with country tunes and comedy. In one form or another, the Blackwoods have been performing as a family band for over sixty years and are one of Branson's premier gospel groups.

In the evening, Ragtime Lil and Banjo-Banjo crank out toe-tapping melodies. Following this, the rocking and rolling Thunderbird Band comes on and and plays into the night.

The Thunderbird Theater

Mel Tillis Theater
2527 Highway 248

Renowned country and western performer Mel Tillis delights audiences of all ages as he plays a hobo in his "King of the Road" skit or just sings his greatest hits including "Ruby, Don't Take Your Love to Town," "Detroit City," and "Who's Julie." Tillis, who was named the Country Music Association's Entertainer of the Year in 1976, has become one of the biggest attractions in Branson, mixing his greatest hits with comedy and dancing. This grand 2,700-seat theater is one of Branson's largest and will eventually house a recording and television studio.

Tillis, once one of the reigning country and western music stars, sounds as good today as he did two decades ago. Tillis also earns rave reviews as a comedian. Afflicted with a stutter since he was a young boy, he has turned it into an advantage and constructed his comedy routine around it. His group of backup singers, incidentally, is called the Stutterettes!

In addition to Mel Tillis, longtime singing star Brenda Lee will be a featured attraction in the coming years.

The Mel Tillis Theater is open March through December.

Bobby Vinton Blue Velvet Theater
2701 76 Country Boulevard

This 1,600-seat theater, all done up in blue, showcases 1950s pop star Bobby Vinton, who performs his top hits including "Blue Velvet," "Roses Are Red," "Mr. Lonely," "Blue on Blue," and "I Love How You Love Me." A former Las Vegas and Atlantic City nightclub performer, Vinton is now accompanied by his mother, son, and two daughters. Vinton charms and entertains, often mingling with members of the audience.

The timeless and always entertaining Glen Miller Orchestra performs its top big band hits of decades ago such as "Chattanooga Choo Choo" and "Moonlight Serenade," "In the Mood," and "Sentimental Journey."

The theater is open April through December.

Waltzing Waters Theater
3616 76 Country Boulevard

The Waltzing Waters Theater features Frederick and the Fountains of Forever. World-class pianist Frederick Antonio performs amid 40,000 gallons of dancing water and a sophisticated light show. A native of the Netherlands, Frederick plays the world's favorite melodies on two concert grand pianos at the same time.

Lawrence Welk Champagne Theater
1984 Highway 165, 3 miles south of Highway 76

Located in the Welk Resort complex, the Champagne Theater is designed to look exactly like the famous television stage from which the *Lawrence Welk Show* broadcast for so many years. The Branson performance is based on the long-running musical variety show and offers great music, nostalgia, the ever-present bubbles, and a friendly ambience.

The Lennon Sisters, the singing group made famous on the long-running *Lawrence Welk Show*, also perform regularly at the theater and are accompanied by the talented twenty-piece Welk Orchestra.

The late bandleader's son, Larry, manages the entire Welk operation.

An award-winning Lennon Brothers Breakfast Show features classic music of the swing era, pianist Jo Ann Castle, and others. The Lawrence Welk Champagne Theater, which seats 2,300, is combined with a marvelous hotel and is open April through December.

Wild West Theater
210 North Gretna Road at Highway 76

The Wild West Theater offers a glitzy, rhinestone- and sequin-filled tribute to the American West. Fun-filled numbers with dancing, singing, and comedy keep audiences enthralled.

The Notorious Hughes Brothers' morning show features rich harmonies, lively singing, and comedy.

The feature attraction of this fine theater is The Great American Wild West Show, an entertaining spectacle for all ages, which includes singing, dancing, costumes, and comedy.

The Wild West Theater is open April through December.

Andy Williams Moon River Theater
2500 76 Country Boulevard

The multimillion-dollar 2,054-seat Andy Williams Theater formally opened in 1992. Inside the theater between the entrance and the lobby, visitors encounter an artificial stream flowing through the building, the "Moon River." The walls are hung with impressive pieces of art from Williams' own collection.

Williams, noted for his super hits "Moon River" and "Days of Wine and Roses," is the consummate performer and enthralls his audiences. His look, manner, and delivery are reminiscent of his award-winning television program that ran for eight years during the late 1960s and early 1970s.

Williams was the first non-country and western artist to move to Branson and become a huge success, paving the way for Bobby Vinton and others.

Andy Williams Moon River Theater

Backed by an eleven-piece orchestra, choir, and dancers, Williams' show is both mellow and rollicking. Williams performs April through December.

Yakov's American Pavilion
1940 Highway 165

One of America's favorite stand-up comedians is Yakov Smirnoff. Performing in a spectacular entertainment complex, this Russian-born funnyman delights one and all in a full, multimedia variety extravaganza. Nonstop laughter is what is to be expected here.

Smirnoff performs February through December.

Yakov's American Pavilion

Theme Parks

Branson has more theme parks for its population and probably per square mile than any other city in America, or for that matter, the world. Four entertainment-filled theme parks are located here in this Ozark town with a population of only 4,000 permanent residents!

Each of the theme parks—Mutton Hollow, Shepherd of the Hills, Silver Dollar City, and White Water—offers an incredibly wide variety ranging from music to crafts to dining to swimming.

Mutton Hollow Entertainment Park and Craft Village

Mutton Hollow opened its doors to the public for the first time in 1970 and has been adding attractions and visitors by the thousands ever since. Mutton Hollow is the hollow where the Old Shepherd, in *The Shepherd of the Hills* by Harold Bell Wright, actually grazed his flock. The setting in this natural hollow is picturesque, the beauty augmented by the park's architecture and landscaping.

Mutton Hollow is located on Highway 376 just west of Highway 76. The park is open seven days a week from the weekend following Easter through the month of October. During the winter, the park remains open only on weekends. Winters, by and large, are comparatively mild in southwestern Missouri, and as a result more and more visitors are coming to Branson and Mutton Hollow to enjoy and participate in the numerous seasonal events and activities.

Admission to Mutton Hollow is free! Each of the special musical performances and other attractions, however, have a moderate fee, with the prices ranging from $2 for pony rides up to $21 for a lunch and musical show.

Parking is never a problem at Mutton Hollow, and the huge parking lot is but a short walk from the main gate.

Inside the park, a principal attraction is the Harold Bell Wright Museum. The museum was established in 1984 by Harold Bell Wright's youngest son, Norman, and contains numerous Wright-related artifacts. The original manuscript of *The Shepherd of the Hills* can be seen here.

Visitors can watch a half-hour film about the life of Harold Bell Wright. The film, incidentally, was produced and directed by Norman Wright, who once worked at the Walt Disney Studios. Norman Wright also narrates a short sound-tour of the museum.

The museum is open seven days a week from mid-April to the last week in October, and is well worth a visit.

Live music can be heard throughout the park as individuals and groups perform a variety of songs and tunes ranging from mountain music to contemporary. It is not unusual to find crowds gathered at the various performances, clapping and singing along. Some visitors have been seen breaking out in a spontaneous dance!

A morning theater, featuring singer Larry Musgrave, begins at 8:30 A.M. and features a sumptuous breakfast feast accompanied by the entertaining music and impressions of Musgrave.

The luncheon show features the Platters Monday through Saturday. This successful singing and recording group of the 1950s, along with other acts, take diners through a nostalgic journey with the music of decades ago. The Platters also perform at 7:00 P.M.

A variety of craft shops line the route as folks wind their way through the park. Here, one can find shops featuring candles, woodworking, stained glass, quilts, and much, much more. At many of them, visitors can actually watch craftsmen fashion the goods that are on sale.

Exciting amusement park-style rides are also found here at Mutton Hollow, including a roller coaster, a Ferris wheel, and a stunning antique merry-go-round.

Other features associated with the grand Entertainment and Craft Village include trail rides, a glowing tribute to America's military veterans, and an annual car show.

For information write to Highway 76, Branson, or call (417) 334-4947.

Shepherd of the Hills Homestead and Outdoor Theater

The Shepherd of the Hills Homestead and Outdoor Theater is located approximately one mile west of Branson on 76 Country Boulevard. The site is on Inspiration Point, a hill that looks out over Mutton Hollow and the Ozark Mountains beyond.

The entrance to the Shepherd of the Hills theme park

The highlight of the Shepherd of the Hills park is, of course, the play. A visit to Branson is not entirely complete unless this spectacular presentation is experienced. This magnificent performance is held each night and features scores of actors and actresses and at least twenty horses. This action-packed play offers gunfights, music, and dancing, some of which can involve the audience!

One particularly noteworthy attraction of the park is the jeep tour, which takes visitors through the woods, to Old Matt's Cabin, and to the incredibly spacious amphitheater. Also available are exciting train rides, wagon rides, and horseback rides.

The park also contains a gift shop, a sweet shop, and Aunt Mollie's Restaurant. (Aunt Mollie, by the way, is one of the main characters in the play.)

Figurine gallery at the Shepherd of the Hills theme park

The Remember When Show at the Shepherd of the Hills theme park

A visit to Shepherd of the Hills park is not complete without a stop at Inspiration Tower. This 230-foot tower weighs over three million pounds and cost over $1.5 million to construct. Visitors can ride to the spacious observation deck at the top in elevators. There, they will witness one of the most spectacular views of the Ozark Mountains. A gift shop, snack bar, and restrooms are located at the base of the tower.

There is no admission fee to the park. Individual attractions, rides, tours, musical programs, and the famous *Shepherd of the Hills* play have separate costs, all of them quite reasonable and affordable for the entire family.

Shepherd of the Hills Homestead and Outdoor Theater is open the last week of April through the month of October. It reopens for the Christmas season where special seasonal entertainment is presented.

For tickets and information, write to Shepherd of the Hills, 5586 West Highway 76, Branson, Missouri 65616, or call 1-800-OLD-MATT,

Silver Dollar City

Silver Dollar City formally opened in 1960 but, in truth, operated as a commercial enterprise many years prior to that time.

During the early 1900s, visitors to nearby Marvel Cave would stop at the small community near the entrance. The town was called Marmaros, and even though the population was rather small, it boasted a hotel, a mercantile, and even a potter.

Marmaros eventually succumbed to the depressed economics of the time and place and no longer exists. During the 1950s, a local woman named Mary Herschend constructed a rustic-looking village reminiscent of an old-timey Ozarks settlement. Some area crafts were sold, and visitors could actually watch soap being made and chair bottoms being caned. In time, the tiny village became something of an entertaining distraction for folks coming to see the cave. Eventually, a lot of visitors started coming just to experience the charm of the little town.

Once a tradition of stopping at this little community became established, profits were made, the village grew, and Mrs. Herschend's two sons opened what they named Silver Dollar City in 1960. It was a propitious move, for around this time the waters backing up to make Table Rock Lake removed a number of farmers from their bottomlands. Since the timber in the area had been cut long ago (see History, Section Four) there appeared to be very little for the hillfolk to do to earn a decent living.

Mrs. Herschend, realizing most of the people possessed certain skills that complemented her little Ozark village, put them to work making furniture, musical instruments, clothes, bonnets, and brooms—all of the things that out-of-staters wanted to purchase and take back home with them as souvenirs and gifts.

Silver Dollar City is grandly appealing in a number of ways. For one thing, it is spotless, and the many flower-beds add a certain classy charm to the operation. The entertainment is also clean and wholesome and a treat for the entire family and people of all ages.

On arriving at Silver Dollar City, the visitor is encouraged to stop at the Hospitality House at the entrance to learn about the park's many activities and attractions and to pick up a map. A casual stroll through the park is fun, entertaining, and quite educational.

Silver Dollar City also has a number of exciting rides. Children and adults love the Lost River of the Ozarks, a thrilling rubber raft ride down the park's river. The roller coaster at Silver Dollar City is unlike roller coasters found anywhere else. Thunderation, as it is called, simulates a string of runaway ore-mining cars that have somehow gotten loose and offers all of the thrills and chills of a top-flight ride.

A ride on the park's train, pulled by a real steam locomotive, is also great fun. The Silver Dollar Steam Train takes visitors on a twenty-minute tour through the park and the nearby Ozark forest. The train even gets stopped and robbed at one point!

There is also a carousel, a small version of a roller coaster suitable for tiny children, a ballroom, and a set of nets and ropes just for kids to climb around on.

One of the newest features at Silver Dollar City is "The World's Largest Treehouse at Geyer Gulch."

As with most of Branson, music is one of the highlights of Silver Dollar City. The Silver Dollar Saloon provides a dance hall ambience, the Opera House seats just over 1,000 for its patriotic performance "American Spirit," and country music can be heard at the Dockside Theater. There are at least fifty musical performances daily!

At night, the Echo Hollow Amphitheater is the setting for a two-hour tribute to Ozark music and culture.

Culture is preserved at Silver Dollar City in a number of different ways. McHaffie's Pioneer Homestead is an authentic Ozark log cabin, and visitors are treated to the actual process of making shingles as well as the shaping and notching of the logs. Visitors get to talk with the craftsmen and artisans, and every once in a while a guest gets to take a few cuts at a log with an axe!

The cabin was originally constructed in 1843 at a location approximately twenty miles away near Forsythia. It was eventually donated to Silver Dollar City by the last owner, Opal Parnell, and moved to its present site.

Arts and crafts make up a significant part of the attractions at Silver Dollar City. Crafts including blown glass, brooms, iron works, leathercraft, and original artwork are available here. At Hazel's Blown Glass Factory, visitors can watch as artisans fashion everything from Christmas tree ornaments to milk glasses.

For those who work up an appetite while wandering about the environs of Silver Dollar City, a number of impressive restaurants are available and accessible. The Bayou Market offers Cajun-style cooking regarded as some of the best to be found outside of Louisiana. Elmer's Frankfurters is a favorite of SDC tourists, and the offerings here remind us how good hot dogs can be!

The Riverside Ribhouse offers barbecue specialties ranging from racks of ribs to a selection of delicious sandwiches. For those who cannot pass up a good pastry shop, Eva and Delilah's Bakery tempts the visitors with luscious aromas and delicious fare. There is also an old-time ice cream parlor and a candy factory.

In addition to all of the above attractions, Silver Dollar City is also the home of a number of important festivals that attract participants throughout the year (see Section Sixteen, Festivals).

For information and tickets, write to Silver Dollar City, HC 1, Box 791, Branson, Missouri 65616 or call 1-800-952-6626.

White Water

White Water is a twelve-acre park located at 3505 76 Country Boulevard. It is open seven days per week, Memorial Day through Labor Day from morning until night.

White Water features twelve different water rides, including a wave pool where the swimmer can actually body surf. There is also a 200-foot-plus triple-drop water slide called the Paradise Plunge.

Other attractions in the park include tournament-quality volleyball courts and clean, well-kept snack bars.

White Water is safety conscious, and Red Cross-trained lifeguards are in abundance here. Life jackets and tubes are available for those who need them.

In recent years, White Water has become a favored place for parents to kick back and relax while their kids enjoy the attractions here. The prices are reasonable, the park is spotless, and the staff is friendly and courteous.

For information and tickets, write to White Water, 3505 76 Country Boulevard, Branson, Missouri 65616 or call (417) 334-7487.

Section Nine

Outdoor Recreation

The Ozark Mountain outdoors of southwestern Missouri have long been associated with hunting, fishing, camping, and hiking. Indeed, long before this region was associated with the wide variety of musical offerings, it was well known throughout much of the United States as a sportsman's haven. With the growth of Branson and the surrounding region as a vacationer's paradise, coupled with the construction of several large reservoirs along the White River, this area is rapidly gaining a national reputation as one of the premier fishing locations in America.

Along with the growth of fishing, the related growth of camping facilities and other outdoor recreational opportunities have lured tens of thousands of outdoor enthusiasts to this area. There is a lot of everything here: fishing, camping, hunting, all kinds of boating, hiking, backpacking, golf, scenic driving, and outdoor photography. Combine these activities with the Branson opportunities for entertainment, musical attractions, theme parks, dining, and shopping, it is easy to see why this region has become a favored destination for millions.

Lake Fishing

The entire region that comprises the Ozark Mountains contains eighteen reservoirs, which cover over 534,000 acres and a combined shoreline of over 7,300 miles! Some of the most picturesque lakes, as well as those offering important fishing, boating, and other water sport opportunities, are located within a short drive from Branson.

Fishermen arrive in the Ozarks to take part in the nationally renowned fishing that has come to be associated with the Ozarks. With the growth of fish hatcheries, along with the stocking of different species of trout in the waters of the White River, the Ozarks has supplanted the Rocky Mountains as the trout fishing capital of North America. The world record brown trout (40 lbs., 4 oz.) was caught in the tailwaters of Arkansas' Greers Ferry Lake.

In addition to trout, fishermen pursue white bass, black bass, stripped bass, crappie, walleye, catfish, and even non-game fish such as carp, sucker, buffalo, drum, and gar.

Lake fishing yields large catches during the autumn, winter, and spring season. While the fishing is still impressive, it falls off somewhat during the summer because of the oxygen depletion that occurs in the lower depths of the lake, a process that results in reduced feeding.

A fog-shrouded White River below Table Rock Dam

Some Fishing Guidelines

Some guidelines for fishing in Branson area lakes are offered here, all contributed by a number of successful local fishermen:

1. Try fishing as soon as possible after a warm rain, especially where feeder streams enter the lake. Don't waste your time fishing during or immediately after a cold rain—the fish are simply not going to bite.
2. Fishing is best during a full moon, as well as during the first and last quarters of the moon.
3. Always fish into the wind.
4. Try fishing when the barometer is on the rise. Fishing is generally best when the barometric reading is 30.00.
5. Fishermen have better luck during cloudy days than during sunny days.
6. Regular lake fishermen claim that fishing immediately following the passage of a cold front yields significant catches.
7. Fishing deep water works best between 10:00 A.M. and 3:00 P.M.
8. Red-colored baits work best in the spring; white-colored baits work best during the autumn.

While a selection of artificial lures have proven successful on Branson-area lakes, live bait continues to provide the best results. Since worms, minnows, grubs, crickets, grasshoppers, and crawfish represent a large percentage of the normal diet of the fish found in these lakes, they continue to be the most successful baits.

The Fish

The most popular fish (and, some say, the easiest to catch) in the Branson-area lakes is the white bass. The white bass offers the sportsman a bit of a challenge, as well as providing a delicious flesh, whether fried, broiled, or baked.

White bass are easily taken during their spring spawning run. An experienced guide can tell you when and where the runs occur. If you don't wish to employ a guide, just watch for the clusters of eager fisherman on the lake pulling these fighting fish from the waters— that's where the action will be!

White bass respond well to jigs, minnows, spinners, and spoons. Fishing from the shore appears to be just about as effective in catching white bass as does fishing out in the lake from boats.

Black bass is a favorite of hard-core fishermen. Three species of black bass are found in Branson-area lakes: the smallmouth, the spotted (or Kentucky), and the largemouth. More largemouth are caught than any of the other two species. Jigs, crank baits, spinners, and plastic worms have proven most effective for catching black bass. Late spring appears to be the best time to fish for these tasty fish.

Crappie fishing is growing in popularity throughout the American South and in the Ozark Mountains. Crappie fishing is definitely on the increase in Branson-area lakes, with stringers of forty or more being seen in recent years.

Local crappie fishermen claim these tasty fish respond well to minnows and gizzard shad, but they will also go after white and yellow jigs. Crappie can be found in large numbers in weeds, brush piles, and submerged trees.

Walleye fishing is also drawing large numbers of adherents to the Branson-area lakes, especially during March and April when these fish are known to spawn. Fishing the shoals during late evening often yields the biggest catches, according to one successful guide. Jig fishing and trolling are the best methods for catching walleye.

Catfish species found in Branson area lakes include channel cat, blue cat, and flathead. As scavengers and bottom feeders, they respond most favorably to chicken livers, frogs, crawfish, dough baits, and stink bait.

Trout fishing is becoming more and more popular on Lake Taneycomo and requires a different set of baits and lures. While fly-fishing is often successful, most of the trout here are taken with salmon eggs, marshmallows, corn, and selected artificial lures.

The Lakes

Beaver Lake

Beaver Lake is located approximately thirty-five miles southwest of Branson. Constructed between 1960 and 1966, the lake covers over forty-two square miles and has an estimated 550 miles of shoreline. The streams draining into Beaver Lake flow over relatively clean limestone and dolomite, consequently the waters tend to be clear.

Beaver Lake regularly yields impressive catches of white bass, black bass, bluegill, crappie, walleye, and catfish.

Bull Shoals Lake

Bull Shoals Lake is located just a short distance to the southeast of Branson and is easily accessible in only ten minutes by car from downtown. The U.S. Army Corps of Engineers lake was completed in 1951 and contains approximately seventy-two square miles of water. Over twenty parks, with camping facilities, can be found around the lake.

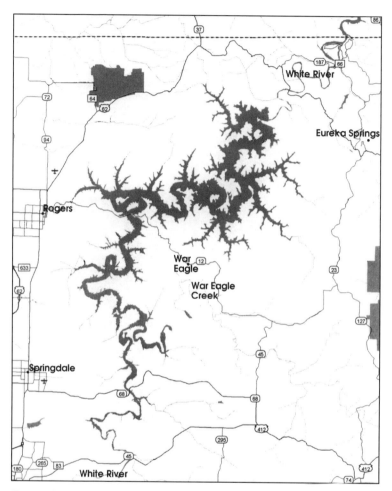

Beaver Lake

Bull Shoals Lake, year round, has remained one of the most popular Ozark lakes with area fishermen as well as regular visitors. Black bass and white bass represent the most popular fishing here, but crappie, channel catfish, and walleye are also popular.

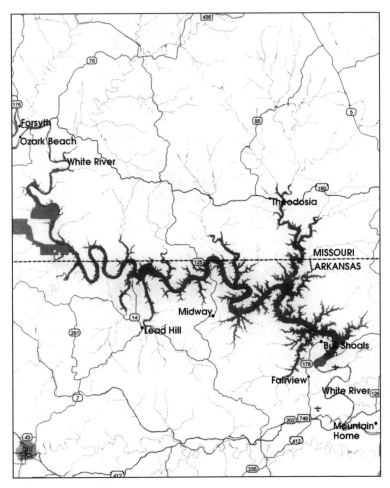

Bull Shoals Lake

Grand Lake of the Cherokees

Eighty miles west of Branson and in the picturesque Ozark environment in the neighboring state of Oklahoma is the Grand Lake of the Cherokees. Impounded by Pensacola Dam, Grand Lake, as it is known by the locals, was formed in 1941, covers over ninety-two square miles, and offers well over 1,200 miles of shoreline.

Like most of the Ozark Lakes, Grand Lake is famous among fishermen throughout most of the country, and the nearby towns of Grove, Jay, Langley, Disney, Pensacola, Ketchum, and Bernice depend, in large part, on tourism related to fishing.

The Grand Lake Shoreline is also similar to other Ozark lakes in a number of ways, offering numerous coves, arms, bluffs, pastureland, and forest. While black bass, white bass, catfish, and bream are regularly taken here, crappie remains the most popular fishing offered by Grand Lake.

Norfork Lake

Norfork Lake is located just a few short miles east of Bull Shoals Lake. Construction on this impoundment was completed in 1944, and the 216-foot tall, 2,624-foot long dam holds back thirty-five square miles of water.

Bass, crappie, walleye, bream, and catfish draw fishermen from all across the United States year round. Norfork Lake is also growing in popularity as a night-fishing location, and throughout most of the year, night-times often find the lake filled with boats outfitted with lights.

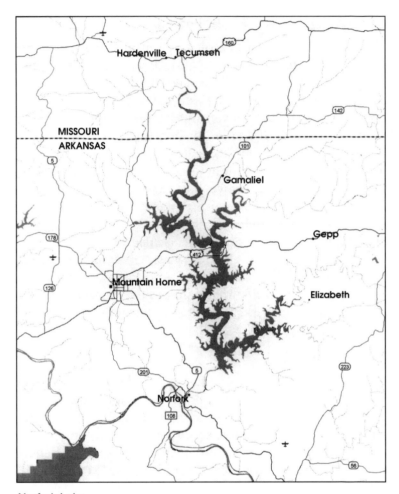

Norfork Lake

Pomme de Terre Lake

Pomme de Terre Lake is approximately a one-hour drive north of Branson. Located just west of Highway 65, Pomme de Terre Lake is a popular spot for area fishermen. Completed in 1961, the lake covers about twelve square miles.

Winding through the Ozark Mountains like a wide river (Pomme de Terre Lake is actually a dammed-up portion of the Pomme de Terre River), this body of water is considered a good spot for bass fishing (white and black), crappie, and catfish.

Stockton Lake

Stockton Lake is a U.S. Corps of Engineers project that was completed in 1969 and is located approximately one hour and fifteen minutes northwest of Branson. The dam is 5,100 feet long and holds back thirty-eight square miles of lake water.

Stockton Late offers a number of recreational opportunities, with fishing clearly the most popular. Black bass, catfish, crappie, and walleye are the favorite catches.

In addition to fishing, hunting has become a very popular activity around Stockton Lake. Nearby publicly owned lands attract waterfowl hunters not only from Missouri, but also from other parts of the Midwest. For information, contact the Missouri Department of Conservation.

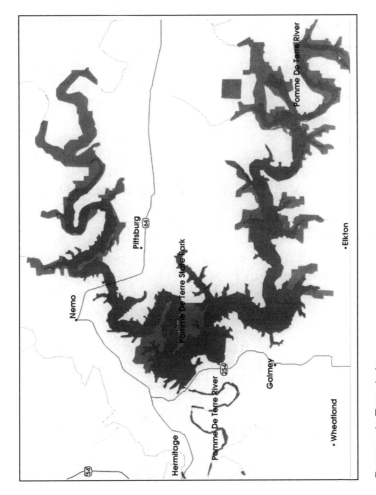

Pomme de Terre Lake

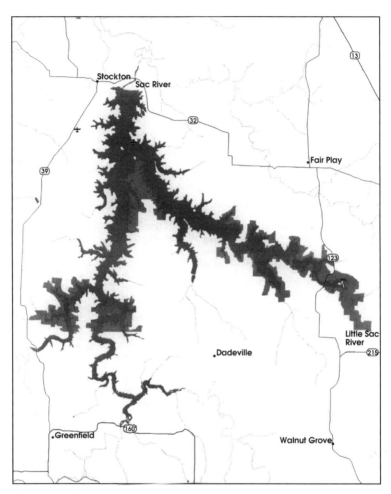

Stockton Lake

Table Rock Lake

Table Rock Dam impounds a portion of the White River to form Table Rock Lake, a large reservoir only a few minutes' drive from Branson. The 6,520-foot long, 252-foot high dam was completed in 1958, and provided for sixty-seven square miles of lake and 745 miles of shoreline.

Table Rock Lake is widely known as a bass, bluegill, and crappie fishing hot spot. Catfishing is also quite popular here, with stringers of eight to ten commonly seen. Shore fishing, as well as boat fishing, has proven popular and productive in this lake, and the numerous coves and arms (where the rivers enter) offer what some sportsmen claim is the best crappie fishing in the United States.

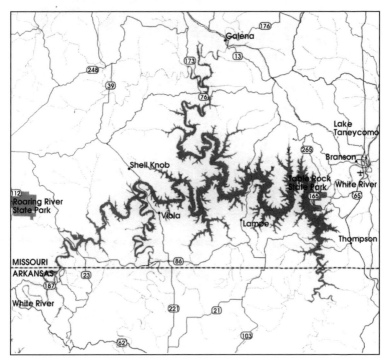

Table Rock Lake

Table Rock Lake offers numerous boat ramps and camping facilities.

One of the marinas at Table Rock Lake

Lake Taneycomo

The long, narrow stretch of the White River known as Lake Taneycomo contains waters backed up by the Powersite Dam, constructed in 1913. So narrow is Lake Taneycomo that many first-time visitors to Branson are initially hesitant to believe it is actually a lake. Until the middle of the twentieth century, this lake—at the time a warm water lake—was a favored fishing area. With the completion of Table Rock Lake in 1958, however, the thermal characteristics of Lake Taneycomo changed significantly: Cold water from the bottom of Table Rock Lake entered Lake Taneycomo, dropping the lake's temperature dramatically. As a result, the colder temperature inhibited the swimming and associated water sports that were pursued at resort areas such as Rockaway Beach and Branson. Furthermore, several species of warm water

117

fish that thrived here were killed off, but the lake eventually evolved into an important trout habitat. These days, the Branson and Rockaway Beach shorelines are filled with eager trout fisherman. Fly-fishing, spin casting, and bottom fishing often yield outstanding results.

The Shepherd of the Hills Trout Hatchery, located adjacent to the Powersite Dam, raises rainbow trout which are, in turn, stocked in the lake. Given the nature of the amphipod population in Lake Taneycomo, this favorite diet of the rainbow trout serves as a nutritious source of food for this fine-tasting fish. Six- to eight-pound rainbows are regularly taken from the lake. The record rainbow weighed fourteen pounds, seven ounces, and was taken in 1976.

While the cooler months of the year are best for taking rainbows, the trout fishing remains good throughout the entire year. Worms, spinners, and jigs, used from shorelines, docks, and boats, are the most popular fishing methods. In recent years, fly-fishermen have reported impressive success along the shorelines.

A fisherman on Lake Taneycomo.

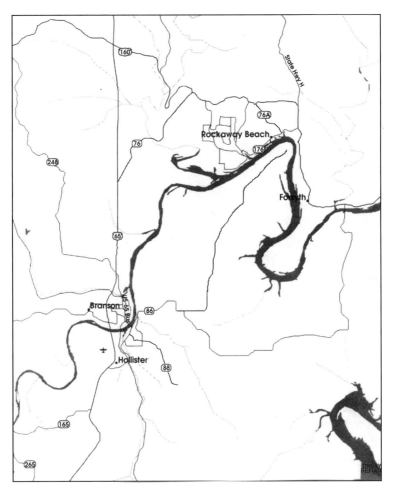

Lake Taneycomo

Harry S. Truman Reservoir

A two-hour drive north and slightly west of Branson will bring fishermen to Harry S. Truman Reservoir, fed largely by the waters of the Osage River and its tributaries.

Completed during the 1970s, the reservoir was named for the late president Truman, who was from Lamar, Missouri. The lake covers over eighty-six square miles and offers over 950 miles of shoreline.

Many who visit Truman Reservoir believe it to be among the most beautiful of the Ozark lakes. The shoreline varies from pastureland to steep-sided, photogenic, tree-covered bluffs.

A relatively young lake that covers portions of six Missouri counties, Truman Reservoir provides a number of different fishing environments favoring black bass, white bass, bream, crappie, catfish, and walleye. A number of accesses enable visitors to fish in virtually every part of the reservoir.

Fishing the Tailwaters

A tailwater is defined as the stretch of river that flows downstream from a dam. In the Branson area of the Ozarks, a number of significant tailwaters offer some of the finest and most productive trout fishing waters in the United States and also produce some world record fish.

The best tailwaters for trout fishing are those associated with Beaver Lake, Bull Shoals Lake, Table Rock Lake, and Norfork Lake

Beaver Lake Tailwaters

The Beaver Lake tailwaters, which extend approximately eight miles downstream from Beaver Dam, are regarded by fishermen as the most important in the White River system. These tailwaters were the first to have trout fishing regulations applied to them, which includes a sixteen-inch minimum length and a daily creel limit of two brown trout, two cutthroat trout, and no limit or size restriction on rainbow trout. These regulations were subsequently applied to the tailwaters of Bull Shoals Lake and Norfork Lake.

The Beaver Lake tailwaters also serve as a site for a habitat restoration activity that many claim will have a significant influence on other trout fisheries.

Fishing for trout in the Beaver Lake tailwaters is regarded as some of the finest anywhere. Particularly successful are micro jigs, crankbaits, and flies. Here and there along the shores of the tailwaters and in nearby towns, the owners of bait and fly shops, cafes, and resorts freely volunteer information on what the fish are biting.

Bull Shoals Tailwaters

Excellent trout habitat extends a total of 101 miles from the dam, and every bit of it is fished by enthusiastic trout fishermen who are drawn here from just about every state in the Union.

Over one million rainbow trout are stocked in these tailwaters each year. In addition to rainbows, one can find cutthroat trout and brown trout. It is the rare fisherman who comes away from these tailwaters without a full catch. The daily limit is similar to that of Beaver Lake.

The Bulls Shoals tailwaters offer a number of advantages and delights to the fisherman. For one thing, it is regarded by many as one of the prettiest stretches of the fishing streams in the country, and the boat-bound angler who prefers to simply drop a line in the water and lazily drift downstream will be treated to some stunning scenery along the way. When this portion of the White River was originally explored during 1819, an observer noted that it is "one of the most beautiful and enchanting rivers who discharge their waters into the Mississippi."

A noted trout biologist once claimed the Bull Shoals tailwater is "unsurpassed," and stated that it is "the best brown trout stream in the world."

Fly fishing the Bulls Shoals tailwaters generally yields impressive catches. Over the years, the most effective flies have been sowbugs, scuds, red butts, beadhead hare's ear nymphs, sulfur duns, sculpins, wooly buggers, midges, hoppers, and shad streamers. Check local establishments for which fly is working best for the season you are visiting.

In addition to flies, trout fishermen claim huge successes with worms, crayfish, and a variety of jigs.

Table Rock Lake Tailwaters

According to noted fisherman and writer Steve Wright, no other fishery in the White River system comes close to that of Lake Taneycomo in terms of trout stocked per mile. In 1993, says Wright, 760,000 trout were stocked in the twenty-two-mile Table Rock Lake tailwaters (which include Lake Taneycomo). The result, fishermen happily report, is an excellent chance to snag some nice-looking trout.

In spite of the fact that the town of Branson attracts over five million tourists per year, many of them fishermen, the tailwaters of Table Rock are a long way from being crowded with anglers.

The Table Rock tailwaters are stocked with rainbows and browns. Steelheads were last stocked in 1975. The daily limit here is five. Only a single brown trout is allowed, and it has a twenty-inch minimum.

Depending on the season, fly fishermen will find scuds and shad imitators particularly effective in the Table Rock tailwaters. Worms and crawfish have also yielded great results.

Norfork Tailwaters

Although there are only slightly less than five miles of Norfork tailwaters before the North Fork River's confluence with the White River, many trout fishermen consider this short stretch of water one of the most important in the Ozark region.

Rainbows, cutthroats, and browns are regularly stocked in the Norfork tailwaters, and in 1994 over 135,000 trout were placed in the stream.

The daily limit in the Norfork tailwaters is six, including not more than two browns and two cutthroats, both with sixteen-inch minimums. The rainbow trout carry no minimum length restrictions.

Jigs, worms, and crawfish work well in the Norfork tailwaters. Fly fishermen have reported successes using woolly buggers and emergers.

In August 1988 a thirty-eight-pound, nine-ounce brown trout was caught on a marshmallow!

Hunting

The first human beings to enter the Ozark Mountains came to hunt. A number of plains and woodland Indian tribes made annual journeys to the Ozarks to hunt deer, elk, bear, and a variety of game birds.

One of the initial attractions to the earliest white settlers in this region was the abundance of wild game. More often than not, the early settlers survived on the bounty of game offered by the rich forests.

Eventually, the area gained a reputation for hunting. Not only were the tables of the area residents heaped high with the meat of wild animals, but the region became a favorite for sport hunting as well as market hunting. During a period of expanding population between 1850 and 1875, hunting pressure became noticeable and a number of species were eliminated from the region. Once plentiful but now extinct in much of the Ozark Mountains were the passenger pigeon, bison, grizzly bear, black bear, elk, wolves, and ivory-billed woodpeckers.

In addition to hunting pressure, habitat modification relative to enhancing agricultural productivity changed many natural environments into man-made ones, thus forcing the native species to move elsewhere.

Between 1875 and 1900, game management, though embryonic in form and practice, was being developed and legislated. Eventually, game limits and hunting seasons for deer, turkey, quail, and prairie chicken were established. Immediately after 1900, conservation and wildlife management agencies were established, their aims oriented toward preserving habitats and species and allowing for continued quality hunting.

Today, the Ozarks, particularly in the Branson region, are famous nationwide for hunting opportunities. Throughout the Ozarks can be found two national forests and approximately forty public hunting areas managed by the Arkansas Game Commission, Missouri Conservation Commission, and the Oklahoma Department of Wildlife Conservation. Maps and information pertaining to hunting areas, along with regulations, may be obtained by writing to these state agencies.

Because so many hunters come to the Ozarks each year in pursuit of game, accommodations are plentiful and range from quality motels to camping facilities (see the section in this chapter on Camping).

Favored game for Ozark hunters include the following:

Deer

As a result of successful game management practices, white-tailed deer are now quite ubiquitous in Ozark forests and are considered by the respective game commissions of Arkansas, Missouri, and Oklahoma to be the most popular animal to hunt. About three-and-a-half feet tall at the shoulder, six feet in length, and weighing anywhere from fifty to three hundred pounds, the whitetails have attracted hunters to the region for generations.

The national and state forests provide great opportunities for deer hunting, though some of the best takes place on private land.

Black Bear

Once plentiful throughout the Ozarks, black bear were killed out during the early 1900s. As a result of successful transplanting experiments, small populations of black bear have been reestablished in these mountains. Check local hunting regulations.

Bobcat

This thirty-pound, nocturnal wildcat is often difficult to locate. Sometimes considered a pest as a result of raiding area chicken houses, bobcats were once hunted to near extinction. Today, according to wildlife observers, they are quite plentiful. Check local hunting regulations.

Fox

Both red foxes and gray foxes are found throughout the Ozarks. Many local residents hunt foxes for the pelts, which still bring good prices in the region. Hunting is often accomplished with foxhounds. Public hunting of foxes takes place, but some of the best locations are on private property. Check local regulations.

Raccoon

Raccoon hunting has long been popular in the Ozarks. The most common fur animal in the region, Raccoons are generally hunted at night, with the hunters accompanied by coon dogs trained to hunt these wily animals. Raccoons are often found near water, where they dine on crayfish and frogs, but are also common in dense woods and bottomlands.

Coyote

Because of gradually increasing prices associated with coyote fur, the hunting of this sly canine in the Ozarks has increased significantly in recent years. The coyote is found throughout every part of the Ozarks, where it is considered by farmers and ranchers to be an unwanted predator on chickens and calves. Though its reputation as a menace to livestock is greatly exaggerated, the coyote is still perceived to be a varmint and is ruthlessly pursued.

Squirrel

One of the fastest growing sports in the Ozarks is squirrel hunting. Families and friends fill Ozark campgrounds each year during squirrel season and pursue these active and elusive tree rodents.

Three types of squirrels can be found in the Ozarks: gray squirrels, red (or fox) squirrels, and flying squirrels. Because of their diminutive size and nocturnal habits, tree squirrels are not considered decent game.

Rabbit

Cottontail rabbits have long been hunted by the local Ozark residents to supplement diets.

Turkey

During the season, the Ozark woods are filled with turkey-hunting enthusiasts who delight in the opportunities found here. According to experts, the eastern wild turkey is the most prized game bird found in the Ozark region today.

Around the year 1900, the turkey population had been decimated as a result of unregulated hunting and habitat destruction. The game commissions of Arkansas, Missouri, and Oklahoma successfully experimented with stocking wild birds imported from eastern forests. The results increased the flocks, and each year virtually all of the counties found in the Ozark Mountains have a lively turkey season.

Dove

During hunting season, the roadsides, farms, and open woods of the Ozarks are often filled with hunters seeking to bag their limit of mourning dove, a favored game bird of many. The Ozarks, particularly that portion that includes Branson, have been growing in popularity with visiting dove hunters each year. National forests, public lands, and private lands offer some spectacular dove hunting.

Quail

Statistics suggest that more bobwhite quail are taken each year by hunters than any other game bird in this region. Known for its tasty meat, this popular game bird is found in the national forests and on public and private land.

Camping

For those who like to camp, unlimited possibilities are available in and around the Branson Ozarks. These range from private facilities to campgrounds maintained and operated by the U.S. Corps of Engineers, National Forest Service, National Park Service, as well as those managed and administered by the states of Missouri and Arkansas.

Many visitors to the Branson area prefer to camp rather than stay in motels because of the agreeable climate, the relatively low cost, and the proximity to fishing, water sports, and hunting opportunities.

Most campsites near Branson have facilities for recreational vehicles as well as tent camping. Most have showers and are close to grocery stores and entertainment.

At last count, there were over 5,000 campsites within a two-hour drive from Branson, and more are being constructed every month.

Private Campgrounds

America's Best Campground

The ABC is one of the newest commercial campgrounds in the area and is located only about one-half mile north of Branson on Missouri State Highway 248. The ABC campground boasts over 150 sites with water and electricity. There are also accommodations for tent campers. This campground also offers six air-conditioned cabins, a swimming pool, spa, a recreation room, a meeting room, and a convenience store.

For information write to America's Best Campground, 499 Buena Vista Road, or call 1-800-671-4399.

Branson City Campgrounds

The distinct advantage of the Branson City Campgrounds is that they are located smack in downtown Branson on the shores of Lake Taneycomo. The camper is within walking distance to many fine restaurants, gift shops, and other commercial outlets. City owned, these grounds offer a swimming pool, tennis courts, and even cable television. The two campgrounds contain well over 300 sites—some in the shade, some in the sun.

For information call (417) 334-8857.

Prime campsites right on Lake Taneycomo.

Branson Shenanigans RV Park

Located just behind BoxCar Willie's showplace, the Branson Shenanigans RV Park offers thirty sites with full hookups, cable television, and a clubhouse next to a flowing creek. Because of limited space, reservations are necessary.

For information write to Branson Shenanigans RV Park, 3675 Keeter Street, or call 1-800-338-7275.

Branson View Campground

One of the most popular destinations with campers, the Branson View Campground contains 45 sites, full hookups, a swimming pool, playground, shuffleboard, laundry, a convenience store, and a free pet kennel. Make reservations well ahead of time.

For information call 1-800-992-9055.

Chastain's RV Park

Chastain's RV Park is located close to the Branson action and is only a stone's throw from the Tony Orlando Theater. The park, which has over 200 sites, also features a nice swimming pool, a convenience store, a playground for the kids, a coin-operated laundry, an exercise room, and a meeting room. Two features that are extremely popular with a growing number of visitors are satellite television hookups and a shuttle service to a number of nearby theaters.

For information write to Chastain's RV Park, 397 Animal Safari Road, or call 1-800-467-7611.

Compton Ridge Campground and Lodge

The Compton Ridge complex is one of the first to become established in Branson. Over 225 sites are nicely spaced over eighty-five acres of woodland a short distance from Silver Dollar City.

Geared for the modern day camper/traveler, Compton's offers a fine restaurant, several laundries, a 650-seat conference center, three outdoor swimming pools, one heated indoor pool, tennis court, and pleasant hiking trails.

If you arrive in either May or September, plan to stay for the Old Time Fiddlers Convention, which has been held on the Compton grounds for over two decades. Make reservations early.

For information call 1-800-233-8648.

Jellystone Park's Yogi on the Lake

Located on the shore of Table Rock Lake about five miles south of Branson is Jellystone Park. This national campground franchise appeals to a large number of travelers. In addition to over 100 campsites, Jellystone also offers a motel and a number of cabins.

Year in and year out, Jellystone's marina appeals to fishermen. While the rest of the family is enjoying the sights and sounds of Branson, a number of dads and husbands prefer to rent a boat at the marina and spend the days fishing the lake for bass and crappie.

Kids love Jellystone, especially the cartoon programs, the hayrides, and the swimming pool.

For information call 1-800-353-BEAR.

KOA Musicland Campground

The KOA Musicland Campground is within walking distance to a number of shows and is located a short distance from BoxCar Willie's Theater. A lot of visitors to KOA take advantage of the location and rarely place their car in the Branson traffic during their stay.

KOA Musicland is a spotless, beautifully kept campground that caters only to RV'ers. In the campground one finds a swimming pool, laundry, rec room, and cable TV. KOA also offers valet parking and car rental!

KOA campgrounds are well known and quite popular around the country with RV'ers. If you wish to stay at KOA Musicland, be sure to make your reservations early—a year in advance is not too soon.

For more information write to KOA Musicland Campground, 116 North Gretna Road, Branson 65616, or call (417) 334-0848.

The Old Shepherd's Campground

Located about one mile from the shows and shopping, the Old Shepherd's Campground offers RV hookups and tent sites. The rather densely wooded setting is kept very clean, and many campers like the relative isolation from the hustle and bustle of town.

For more information call 1-800-544-6765.

Pea Patch RV Park

The Pea Patch RV Park is another one of the fine private campgrounds located within walking distance of so many of Branson's fine shows. Catering only to RV'ers, Pea Patch boasts 83 sites, a swimming pool, and laundry. At Pea Patch, you can even get free morning coffee!

For information call (417) 335-3958.

Shadow Rock Park and Campground

Located at the junction of Missouri Highways 76 and 160 near the town of Forsyth, Shadow Rock is within spitting distance of Bull Shoals Lake. Fishing is popular here, as is the swimming pool and an occasional rodeo!

For more information call (417) 546-4763.

Silver Dollar City Campground

As the name suggests, this attractive campground is located close to the noted theme park. A total of 185 sites set in a clean, wooded area greet the arriving camper.

If your travel agenda includes a visit to the Silver Dollar City theme park, you're in luck here, for a regular shuttle service leaves the campground and delivers you right to the front gate!

In the campground are three swimming pools, a nice playground, laundry, game room, and a convenience store.

For more information call 1-800-477-5164.

National Forest Campgrounds

The Mark Twain National Forest covers selected portions of southern Missouri. Three segments of the forest are located within relatively short driving distance to Branson. In addition to campgrounds, the national forests also offer streams for floating, canoeing, and kayaking as well as opportunities for hiking, backpacking, and picnicking.

Maps and information on camping and other features can be obtained by writing to the headquarters for the Mark Twain National Forest, P.O. Box 937, Rolla, Missouri 65401.

North Fork

North Fork Campground is located about fifty miles due east of Branson. The good news is that there is no fee charged to camp here. The bad news is that there are only six campsites. Toilets and drinking water are available, and activities including hiking, fishing, and boating are eagerly pursued by visitors.

Paddy Creek

Located about one-and-a-half hours northeast of Branson, Paddy Creek Campground is most easily reached from Highway 17 north of Roby and four miles east on a Forest Service road. Twenty-three campsites are available. The campground features pit toilets, drinking water, and fishing.

Sycamore

If the North Fork Campground is full when you arrive there, travel just a few miles to the north to Sycamore where you will encounter ten more sites. Sycamore Campground offers much the same as North Fork relative to boating, fishing, and hiking.

United States Army Corps of Engineers Campgrounds

Throughout the United States, the Corps of Engineers provides some of the finest public camping facilities and locations. Well maintained and suitably located for fishing, boating, and picnicking, the COE campgrounds are most often found along lakes.

Beaver Lake

Beaver Lake has ten fine campsites with a variety of facilities. They include: *Beaver Springs* (18 campsites, drinking water, restrooms, swimming, boat ramp); *Dam Site* (78 campsites, drinking water, dump station, electricity, restrooms, boat ramp, swimming); *Hickory Creek* (38 campsites, drinking water, restrooms, showers, dumping stations, boat ramp, swimming); *Horseshoe Bend* (103 campsites, drinking water restrooms, showers, dump station, boat ramp, swimming); *Indian Creek* (42 campsites, drinking water, restrooms, boat ramp, swimming); *Prairie Creek* (119 campsites, drinking water, restrooms, electricity, dump station, boat dock and ramp); *Rocky Branch* (50 campsites, drinking water, restrooms, electricity, swimming, boat ramp and dock); *Starkey* (32 campsites, drinking water, restrooms, electricity, boat dock and ramp); *Ventris* (17 campsites, drinking water, restrooms, boat ramp, swimming); *War Eagle* (22 campsites, drinking water, restrooms, electricity, swimming, boat ramp and dock).

Most of the campsites at Beaver Lake can be reserved by telephone or in person. Otherwise, they are available on a first-come, first-served basis. Collect calls and reservation requests made by mail will not be accepted. To receive a map and more detailed information about camping on Beaver Lake, write or call the Project Manager, P.O. Box 8, Rogers, Arkansas 72756. (501) 636-1210

Bull Shoals Lake

There are eleven prime camping areas with a variety of facilities associated with Bull Shoals Lake. Some of the camping locations are in Missouri, others are in Arkansas. They include: *Beaver Creek* (16 campsites, drinking water, restrooms, dump station, fishing dock, boat rental, bait shop, swimming); *Buck Creek* (34 campsites drinking water, restrooms, electricity, dump station, playground, swimming); *Bull Shoals* (12 campsites, drinking water, restrooms, dump station, boat ramp and dock); *Dam Site* (35 campsites, drinking water, restrooms, dump station); *Highway 125* (32 campsites, drinking water, restrooms, electricity, dump station, playground, swimming, boat ramp and dock); *Highway K* (19 campsites, drinking water, restrooms, boat ramp, boat rental, bait shop); *Kissee Mills* (8 campsites, drinking water, restrooms, boat ramp, picnic tables); *Lake View* (81 campsites drinking water, restrooms, showers, dump station, boat ramp and dock, playground, swimming); *Lead Hill* (78 campsites, drinking water, restrooms, electricity, playground, boat ramp, group shelters, and a heated fishing dock!); *Oakland* (34 campsites, drinking water, restrooms, dump station, boat ramp and dock, swimming); *Ozark Isle* (118 campsites, drinking water, restrooms, showers, group shelter, playground, boat ramp and dock, swimming, group camping); *Point Return* (28 campsites, drinking water, restrooms, dump station, boat ramp, swimming); *Pontiac* (34 campsites, drinking water, restrooms, dump station, boat ramp, boat rentals, swimming); *River Run* (20 campsites, drinking water, restrooms, boat ramp); *Shadow Rock* (16 campsites, drinking water, restrooms, electricity, boat ramp, boat rental, cafe, bait shop); *Spring Creek* (16 campsites, drinking water, restrooms, boat ramp); *Theodosia* (34 campsites, drinking water, restrooms, dump station, electricity, boat ramp, boat rental, cafe, swimming); *Tucker Hollow* (30 campsites, drinking water, restrooms, dump station, boat ramp and dock, swimming).

For a map and more information on the facilities at Bull Shoals Lake, write the Resident Engineer, P.O. Box 369, Mountain Home, Arkansas 72653.

Norfork Lake

There are sixteen camping areas associated with Norfork Lake, each with a variety of facilities. They include: *Bidwell Point* (48 campsites, restrooms, drinking water, electricity, dump station, swimming); *Buzzard Roost* (6 campsites, drinking water, restrooms, boat ramp); *Cranfield* (74 campsites, drinking water, restrooms, electricity, dump stations, swimming, boat rental); *Curley Point* (4 campsites, drinking water only); *Gamaliel* (29 campsites, drinking water, restrooms, dump station, boat ramp, boat rental); *George's Cove* (12 campsites, drinking water, restrooms, boat ramp, swimming); *Hand Landing* (7 campsites, drinking water, restrooms, dump station, boat ramp, swimming, boat rental); *Howard Cove* (14 campsites, drinking water, restrooms, boat rental); *Jordon* (33 campsites, drinking water, restrooms, dump station, electricity, boat dock, swimming); *Panther Bay* (28 campsites, drinking water, restrooms, dump station, boat ramp and dock, swimming); *Pigeon Creek* (5 campsites, drinking water, restrooms, boat ramp and dock); *Red Bank* (12 campsites, drinking water, restrooms, boat ramp); *Robinson Point* (102 campsites, drinking water, restrooms, showers, electricity, dump station, swimming); *Tracy* (7 campsites, drinking water, restrooms, boat ramp); *Quarry Cove and Dam Site* (59 campsites, drinking water, restrooms, dump station, boat dock, swimming); *Woods Point* (11 campsites, drinking water, restrooms, boat ramp).

For a map and more information on the camping areas of Norfork Lake, write or call the Project Manager, P.O. Box 369, Mountain Home, Arkansas 72653. (870) 425-2700.

Table Rock Lake

There are twenty-one prime camping sites along the shore of Table Rock Lake, each offering a variety of facilities. They include: *Aunts Creek* (58 campsites, drinking water, restrooms, swimming, boat ramp, picnic tables); *Baxter* (50 campsites, drinking water, restrooms, showers, sanitary station, boat ramp, picnic tables, bait shop, and boat rental); *Campbell Point* (76 campsites, drinking water, restrooms, showers, sanitary station, trailer hookups, bait shop, boat and motor rental); *Cape Fair* (86 campsites, drinking water, restrooms, sanitary station, boat ramp, boat and motor rental, and cafe); *Cow Creek* (33 campsites, drinking water, restrooms, boat ramp), Eagle Rock (29 campsites, drinking water, restrooms, showers, laundromat, boat ramp, boat rental, bait shop); *Highway 13* (148 campsites, drinking water, restrooms, showers, laundromat, trailer hookups, sanitary station, boat ramp, boat and motor rental, bait shop); *Indian Point* (80 campsites, drinking water, restrooms, sanitary station, trailer hookups, swimming, boat ramp, boat and motor rental, cafe); *Joe Bald* (47 campsites, drinking water, restrooms, boat ramp), Kings River (16 campsites, drinking water, restrooms, boat ramp); *Long Creek* (45 campsites, drinking water, restrooms, swimming, boat ramp, boat and motor rental, bait shop, cafe); *Mill Creek* (61 campsites, drinking water, restrooms, showers, swimming, boat ramp); *Monett Big M* (92 campsites, drinking water, restrooms, showers, sanitary station, trailer hookups, boat ramp, boat and motor rentals, bait shop); *Old Highway 86* (87 campsites, drinking water, restrooms, showers, sanitation station, swimming, boat ramp); *Viney Creek* (41 campsites, drinking water, restrooms, boat ramp); *Viola* (57 campsites, drinking water, restrooms, trailer hookups, boat ramp, boat and motor rentals).

The Visitors Center at Table Rock Dam

One of the many beaches at Table Rock Lake

Reservations for campsites at Table Rock Lake will be accepted only by telephone or in person. For a map and more information about the campsites on Table Rock Lake, write or call the Corps Project Manager, P.O. Box 1109, Branson, Missouri 65616. (417) 334-4101.

Arkansas State Park Campgrounds

Travelers with experience camping in state parks around the country claim Arkansas' park and facilities are second to none. Some of the finest of the Arkansas state parks are located within short driving distance to Branson, Missouri. They include:

Bull Shoals State Park

Bull Shoals State Park is located about forty-five miles southeast of Branson as the crow flies. Nestled ideally on the bank of the White River and just a short distance downstream from the dam at Bull Shoals Lake, this attractive park offers drinking water, restrooms, showers, sanitary dump stations, boat ramp, fishing dock, boat and motor rental, and hiking trails. Long an important location for trout fishermen, this well-kept and ideally located park is close to stores and gas stations.

Withrow Springs State Park

Located about forty miles due southwest of Branson, Withrow Springs State Park appeals to those who prefer a fairly quiet setting away from the hustle and bustle of busy campgrounds. Experienced fisherman also know that nearby War Eagle Creek provides some excellent fishing. Facilities in the park include drinking water, restrooms, showers, swimming pool, tennis courts, and snack bar. The historic Arkansas town of Huntsville, home of the late Arkansas Governor Orval Faubus, is only five miles away.

For more information on Arkansas State Parks, write or call the Arkansas Department of Parks and Tourism, One Capitol Mall, Little Rock, Arkansas 72201. (501) 371-777.

Missouri State Park Campgrounds

Like Arkansas, the state of Missouri maintains many excellent parks ideal for camping, fishing, hiking, and a host of other activities. In the general area of Branson, several parks have proven popular with visitors. They include:

Roaring River State Park

This impressive state park is located only about twenty-five miles west of Branson. The trip from Branson to Roaring River State Park is an enjoyable one that passes through lush Ozark forests and skirts portions of Table Rock Lake.

One of the chief attractions at Roaring River is the spring that brings to the surface over twenty million gallons of water each day, providing the source for the Roaring River. Roaring River, by the way, is a popular trout fishing stream that is stocked on a regular basis from a nearby trout hatchery overseen by the Missouri Department of Conservation.

Roaring River State Park includes over 200 campsites, drinking water, swimming pool, hiking trails, horseback rides, hotel, cabins, restaurant, and store.

Stockton State Park

Stockton State Park is located on Stockton Lake and is about a one-hour drive northwest of Branson. With 83 campsites, this park also features a motel, restaurant, swimming beach, and a boat ramp.

Table Rock State Park

One of the most popular camping destinations for visitors to Branson is Table Rock State Park, located right on the shores of the lake and only about a ten-minute drive from entertainment, restaurants, and shopping. The well-kept park has over 180 campsites and all of the amenities modern campers have come to expect.

The campground at Table Rock State Park

For more information on Missouri State Parks, write or call the Missouri Department of Natural Resources, Parks, and Historic Preservation Division, 1915 Southridge Drive, P.O. Box 176, Jefferson City, Missouri 65102. (314) 751-2479.

Golf

In addition to the wonderful entertainment, the unparalleled shopping, great camping, and some of the country's finest lake and stream fishing, Branson is gaining quite a reputation as a popular golfing center. Golf, in fact, is one of the fastest growing outdoor activities in this vacation paradise, and no less than nine fine golf courses are located in and around Branson. Most of these courses are relatively new, featuring modern design, and all of them offer some exciting challenges.

City of Branson Golf Course

Located on Compton Drive, this seven-acre, nine-hole golf course is located next to the Branson Community Center and is open to the public Monday through Saturday.

Diamond Hills Country Club

Located some thirty-seven miles southeast of Branson, this fine eighteen-hole course regularly attracts visitors to Missouri's entertainment mecca. After paying a moderate fee for the first eighteen holes, the rest of the day is free at the Diamond Hills course. Featured are bent grass greens, riding or pull carts, and even rental clubs. There is also a driving range, and the club restaurant is open seven days a week. With the daily fee, golfers may use all of the clubhouse facilities including the swimming pool.

Diamond Hills Country Club is located in Diamond City, Arkansas. For more information call (870) 422-7613.

Holiday Hills Resort and Golf Club

Long one of the most popular courses with area linksters, this course has recently been redesigned to meet PGA specifications. Featuring bent grass greens and hybrid bermuda fairways and tees, this eighteen-hole championship course is open to the public and offers a fully stocked pro shop, a club repair service, and a snack bar. The full eighteen holes with a cart costs $18.

Holiday Hills Resort and Golf Club is located three miles east of Branson on Missouri Highway 76. For more information call (417) 334-4838.

Kimberling Golf Course

The nine-hole course is a 2,335-yard, par 34 challenge set in a lovely, but somewhat hilly, environment. Open seven days a week, the fee at this writing was only $10 for the nine-hole trip without a cart, which is an extra ten bucks.

The Kimberling Golf Course is located at the intersection of 1 Lakeshore Drive and Highway 13 at Kimberling City. For more information call (417) 739-4370.

Ledgestone Country Club

Golf Digest nominated the Ledgestone course in 1995 as the Best New Golf Course in the country. Designed by Tom Clark, this par 71 course is the favorite of a lot of Branson entertainers, and the visiting golfer can often find one or more of them playing at any given time. This course, it is said, is for the serious and skilled golfer. At this writing, the green fees for eighteen holes was $70, including cart.

Ledgestone Country Club is located at the intersection of Missouri Highways 76 West and 265. For more information call (417) 337-2474 or 1-800-81-STONE.

Oakmont Community Golf Course

Located just a few minutes south of Branson at Ridgedale, this par 36 nine-hole course is described by regulars as "challenging." The challenges come, say those who know, from the sloping hills and narrow fairways.

Ten dollars for the nine-hole course ($10 more for a cart) is very reasonable.

The Oakmont Community Golf Course is located at 2722 Missouri Highway 286. For more information call (417) 334-1572.

Pointe Royale Golf Club

This course, featuring lush fairways and immaculate greens, is the favorite of Branson performer Andy Williams, who lives nearby. Other celebrities often seen here are Moe Bandy, Mickey Gilley, and Charlie Pride. This par 70, eighteen-hole course is the talk of the town, is well known throughout the country, and is located just across from the Lawrence Welk Theater near Lake Taneycomo. The club pro will tell you the greens are very fast, and he has a lot of suggestions to help you better your score on this beautiful course.

The fee for eighteen holes is $60 including the cart. Those staying at the Point Royale resort pay $40 with a cart.

The Pointe Royale Golf Club is located at 142 Pointe Royale Drive. For more information call (417) 334-4477 or 1-800-962-4710.

Taneycomo Golf Club

Located a few minutes west of Branson, the town of Forsyth offers a challenging nine-hole, par 35 golf course. The challenges here come in the form of somewhat small and sloping greens. Regardless, the course is popular with many and charges only $12 for nine holes, carts extra.

Taneycomo Golf Club is located on Missouri Highway 160. For more information call (417) 546-5454.

Thousand Hills Golf Club

Located just two blocks south of the Grand Palace in downtown Branson, Thousand Hills Golf Club is a par 64 eighteen-hole course, open to the public, and has a PGA pro to offer the best advice on how to get through it. The course features bent grass greens and zoysia fairways and tees. At the clubhouse, you will find a golf shop, a snack bar, and a meeting room.

Thousand Hills Golf Club is located at 245 South Wildwood Drive. For information call (417) 334-4553 or 1-800-864-4145.

Top of the Rock Golf Course

From this beautiful forty-seven-acre, nine-hole course atop an Ozark hill, you can see Table Rock Lake below. John Morris, owner of the famous Bass Pro Shops, backed this project, which was designed by golfing great Jack Nicklaus.

The Top of the Rock course has one of the most attractive settings anyone could expect to find in a golf course. In cooperation with the Audubon Society, interpretive markers are found throughout the area.

Top of the Rock also features a "full service" driving range, with artificial and natural surface tee areas, and an excellent pro shop.

For information call (417) 339-5225.

Boating

The wide selection of lakes and streams in and near Branson provide innumerable opportunities for boating of all kinds: sailboating, motorboating, jet skiing, canoeing, rafting, and kayaking.

For those interested in boating on one or more of the lakes, write or call the supervisors associated with any and all of them for specific information relative to facilities, boat docks, and boat ramps.

Project Manager, Beaver Lake
Beaver Lake Project Office
U.S. Army Corps of Engineers
P.O. Box H
Rogers, Arkansas 72756
(501) 636-1210

Project Manager, Bull Shoals Lake
Bull Shoals Lake Project Office
U.S. Army Corps of Engineers
Mountain Home, Arkansas 72653
(870) 425-2700

Project Manager, Norfork Lake
Norfork Lake Resident Office
U.S. Army Corps of Engineers
P.O. Box 369
Mountain Home, Arkansas 72653
(870) 425-2700

Project Manager, Pomme de Terre Lake
Pomme de Terre Lake Project Office
U.S. Army Corps of Engineers
Hermitage, Missouri 65668
(417) 745-6411

Project Manager, Stockton Lake
Stockton Lake Project Office
U.S. Army Corps of Engineers
Route 1
Stockton, Missouri 65785
(417) 276-3113

Project Manager, Table Rock Lake
Table Rock Lake Project Office
U.S. Army Corps of Engineers
P.O. Box 1109
Branson, Missouri 65616
(417) 334-4101

Office Manager, Taneycomo Lake
Empire Electric Co.
Star Route 5, Route 450
Forsyth, Missouri 65653
(417) 546-2111

Ozark Float Streams

The Ozark Mountains that surround the town of
Branson in all directions contain some of the most popular float streams in the country. Canoeists, kayakers,
rafters, and tubers come from every state in the Union, as
well as from a number of foreign countries, to float these
impressive and scenic Ozark waters. These waters, for
the most part spring-fed, remain cool and clear year
round, attracting floaters, fishermen, picnickers, and
others who simply come to enjoy the scenery and the
peace and quiet.

Vacationers love kayaking and canoeing Ozark streams

Some general rules worth following while floating the Ozark streams are: (1) Always wear a personal flotation device; (2) Always check with local officials before undertaking a float trip. Adverse weather and water conditions have ruined many a potentially fine float trip; (3) Respect private property encountered along the trip; (4) Always canoe with others; (5) Transport valuables in a watertight container; (6) Carry along a spare paddle; (7) Only experienced canoeists and kayakers should attempt to run potentially dangerous rapids; (8) Carry along a first aid kit.

Major float streams of the Branson-area Ozarks include:

Beaver Creek

Twenty miles of Beaver Creek—from Jackson Mill to Bull Shoals Lake in Missouri—is regarded by many as one of the most popular and attractive floats in the area. Not only do canoeists and kayakers seek the peace of a quiet float in this incredibly photogenic country, but fishermen prize Beaver Creek for its impressive yields of black bass, white bass, and crappie.

Buffalo National River

Located about forty miles south of Branson in the state of Arkansas, the Buffalo National River is considered one of the prime floating streams in the United States. Administered by the National Park Service, the Buffalo National River is one of the few remaining unspoiled rivers in the country. Its meandering course takes the floater past towering limestone bluffs, clear pools, and some of the most picturesque Ozark scenery anywhere. The lower half of the Buffalo National River can be floated throughout the entire year; the upper half is floatable only during periods of sufficient rainfall.

There are a number of access and egress points along the stretch of stream, and canoe rental establishments abound.

Bull Creek

Bull Creek, which empties into Lake Taneycomo near the town of Forsyth, is a relatively short stream (approximately ten miles long) and can be floated during the rainy seasons of spring and autumn. Bull Creek floaters often combine fishing with their trip and report fine catches of largemouth and smallmouth bass.

Elk River

Year-round floating on southwestern Missouri's Elk River can be experienced downstream from the Indian Creek confluence clear to the Grand Lake of the Cherokees in Oklahoma. Many Elk River enthusiasts turn their float into a two- or three-day camping and fishing expedition. There are a number of excellent campsites along the route, and fishermen report large catches. Many canoeists claim Elk River offers some of the most outstanding Ozark scenery to be found anywhere.

Flat Creek

Like many Ozark streams, Flat Creek is only floatable from the community of Jenkins to Missouri's Table Rock Lake during the wetter spring and autumn seasons. Canoeists report wonderful scenery, a good current without being hazardous, and excellent fishing.

Gasconnade River

The Gasconnade is considered by Missourians as one of the most popular float streams in the state and regularly attracts fishermen from around the country throughout the course of a year to fish for catfish, buffalo, largemouth and smallmouth bass, and sunfish.

The Gasconnade offers nearly three hundred miles of floatable water, numerous campsites, canoe rental enterprises, and a wide selection of access and egress points. Most floaters prefer the upper reaches of the stream for exciting float trips.

James River

For the many years before floaters took their recreational pursuits to the White River, the James River was considered one of the most popular streams in the area for floating and fishing. Make no mistake about it: The James River is still quite popular, and on good days you might see as many as fifty other floaters on this appealing stream. Below Lake Springfield, the James River is a good float throughout the year. Above the lake, however, only the spring and fall seasons offer any kind of significant water.

Dramatic scenery along the James River attracts many floaters to this area. Spectacular limestone bluffs, numerous caves, and a natural bridge bring visitors back to this stream every year.

Access to and egress from the James River is easily accomplished at a number of sites.

Kings River

If you are looking for a bit of a floating challenge, the Kings River may be the stream for you. Stretches of this river can be swift and sometimes even dangerous. Beginners are advised to try the Kings River only after obtaining some experience. According to writer Milton Rafferty, the months between April and June are the best for floating this stream. Below U.S. Highway 62 in Carroll County, Arkansas, the Kings River can be floated after June.

A number of longtime Ozark stream floaters prefer camping along the attractive gravel bars of the Kings River over any other stream, and it is not uncommon to encounter groups of campers along the way.

Little Niangua River

Located only about two hours north of Branson, the Little Niangua River offers a pleasant and sometimes quite exciting thirty-mile float from the bridge on U.S. 54 near the community of Almon downstream to the Missouri J bridge. During the summertime, the Little Niangua River is usually too shallow to offer much of a float. During the wetter spring and fall seasons—the best times to float this stream—the river can provide some serious canoeing adventure. Float fishing along the Little Niangua often yields catches of crappie, channel catfish, and largemouth and smallmouth bass.

Niangua River

In addition to being a fine float stream, the Niangua River, which drains into the Lake of the Ozarks, attracts fishermen year round who reel in fine catches of trout. Spring fed with cool, clear water, the Niangua offers approximately thirty miles of excellent floating from the

Missouri 32 bridge access to the dam near the community of Edith. For those who prefer shorter trips, there are a number of easy access and egress points along the length of the stream. Many floaters camp at Bennett Spring State Park, a short distance downstream from the Missouri 32 bridge.

Osage Fork of the Gasconnade River

The serious canoeist or kayaker can float as much as sixty miles of the Osage Fork during the high water seasons of spring and autumn. This stream offers some spectacular scenery, excellent fishing, and occasionally some challenging water.

Pomme de Terre River

The upper Pomme de Terre River is a favorite float for area residents. The farthest upstream entry is the Sunset Bridge on Missouri Highway Y, but there are a number of access and egress points throughout the forty-mile floatable length of this stream. Best times for floating are spring and fall.

Sac River

The Sac River is an excellent stream for beginning canoeists and kayakers. The gentle gradient and relatively slow flowing water provides for a peaceful float. The middle section of the Sac River that flows between Stockton Lake and Lake of the Ozarks can be floated virtually any time of the year except during extremely dry summer. A twenty-mile portion of the Sac River located above Lake Stockton is floatable throughout the year. Fishing on the Sac River is considered to be good, and impressive catches of channel catfish and bass have been reported.

Shoal Creek

Shoal Creek, a tributary of the White River, is a pleasant float and a fine fishing stream. The shoals, for which it is named, offer thrills without being dangerous, and the beautiful scenery along the way is well worth a day on this stream. Access points along Shoal Creek are numerous and safe.

Spring River

Missouri's Spring River eventually joins Kansas' Neosho River and offers an exciting float. Between the months of October and June, the portion of the stream above Carthage, Missouri, provides a great floating adventure. Below Carthage, the Spring River can be floated throughout the year.

The Spring is not a large stream, and here and there along the route, the floater has to deal with overhanging tree limbs, dense brush growth, and a few slightly challenging shoals.

Over two decades ago, the Spring River was seriously polluted with dioxin, which emptied into the stream from a chemical firm at Verona. To this day, it is recommended that fish taken from this stream not be eaten.

There are numerous access and egress points along the Spring River.

Swan Creek

White-water kayakers and canoeists from all over the Midwest come to Swan Creek during the spring to experience some thrilling white-water floating. When the spring runoff fills Swan Creek the water is very fast, and many experienced kayakers call it "dangerous." It is not uncommon to find boulders and submerged trees in the middle of the stream during a run.

When the rainy season is finished, Swan Creek provides a gentler float, and entire families as well as organized groups are often seen tubing and canoeing this popular river.

White River

From the tiny Arkansas community of Boston, the White River flows into and out of several reservoirs, including Table Rock, Taneycomo, and Bull Shoals. Eventually, this river, popular for both floating and fishing, joins with the Mississippi River.

The best time for floating, according to White River veterans, is from October to early May. The White River provides an exciting, yet comparatively safe, run for all kinds of floaters. Canoeists have been visiting the White River for decades. As kayaking grows in popularity, more and more of these craft are seen on the river.

A float trip down the White River is not complete without some fishing. Long regarded as one of the premier trout fishing streams in both Arkansas and Missouri, if not the entire United States, the White River yields large catches and record-size fish.

More Fun Things To Do

The reputation currently enjoyed by the town of Branson revolves principally around the wide selection of a variety of fine music and related entertainment. Less known, but nonetheless important to many members of visiting families, are the numerous other delightful and entertaining diversions, ranging from go-cart rides to visits to museums.

Indeed, Branson's reputation as an entertainment center is beginning to incorporate every aspect of that term. Below are offered several alternative types of family fun found in Branson, all within easy driving distance and all reasonably priced.

Amusement Centers

Bumper Boats Amusement Center

The most popular ride with the kids here, of course, is the bumper boats. These water vehicles are completely safe and easy to drive. The visitor also can find a bungee trampoline and a simulated rock wall for climbing and rappelling, a challenge for both youths and the parents. Several other rides and games offer entertaining and exciting diversions at Bumper Boats Amusement Center.

Bumper Boats is open seven days a week and is located at 1715 76 Country Boulevard. For more information call (427) 335-2628.

Kids Kountry

Kids Kountry is designed for younger children from kindergarten age through the second grade and offers a nice selection of kiddie rides, including bumper boats and kiddie carts. In addition, there is a miniature golf course that mom and dad and the older kids will enjoy.

Kids Kountry is located at 2505 76 Country Boulevard. For more information call (417) 334-1618.

Pirate's Cove

Two exciting and somewhat different miniature golf courses lure travelers here. Be aware, however, that these are no ordinary courses—they offer challenges to kids and adults alike, challenges not found on any ordinary course.

Pirate's Cove is located at 2901 Green Mountain Drive. For information call (417) 336-6606.

Ridge Runners

Ridge Runners is a popular destination for families visiting Branson, and features go carts with a choice of dirt track, junior Pro-Am track, slick track, and a fast track. In addition, there is an excellent miniature golf course and an arcade with a variety of games.

For information call (417) 335-4085.

Thunder Road

Thunder Road features bumper cars, go-carts, batting cages, a large video arcade, skeeball, bungee trampoline, gyro orbiter, and two eighteen-hole miniature golf courses.

Thunder Road is located at 3235 76 Country Boulevard at Gretna Road, right across from the Osmond Family Theater. For information call (417) 334-5905.

The Track Recreation Centers

The Track has five locations throughout Branson, all of which are open from 9:00 A.M. to 11:00 P.M. Most of The Track locations have go-carts and tracks, as well as miniature golf.

Track Four features the Orbitron, which simulates the movements of an astronaut in space. For pure excitement, try the trampoline and harness arrangement, which helps the beginning jumper perform flips—frontward and backward.

All of The Track's locations are on 76 Country Boulevard and convenient to the entertainment and restaurant strip. For information call (417) 334-1613.

Bass Pro Shop

The forty-five minutes it takes to drive from Branson to Springfield to visit the world-famous Bass Pro Shop and the incredible, educational Wildlife Museum is worth every minute. Bass Pro Shop, the outdoor supply heaven known the world over by fishermen, hunters, campers, and other avid sportsmen, is worth the trip alone, but the 17,000-square-foot Wildlife Museum is certainly an added treat.

At the Wildlife Museum, the visitor will encounter skillfully constructed dioramas portraying native American animals in their natural habitats. Here you can see life-like displays of mountain lion, caribou, buffalo, bighorn sheep, and many, many more examples of wildlife. Also found here are antique fishing rods and reel, lures, boats, and motors.

For more information write to Bass Bro. Shops Outdoor World, 1935 South Campbell, Springfield, Missouri, or call (417) 887-1915.

Lake and River Cruises

The *Lake Queen*

Climb aboard this clean and safe stern-wheeler riverboat and enjoy the fabulous scenery and a great all-you-can-eat buffet as you ply the waters of the White River. From the deck you can watch a variety of wildlife as you pass by scenic bluffs and peaceful coves.

Feel free to get up and dance as the band plays your favorite tunes, or just sit back, relax, and listen to the refrains of the music of times past.

Kids particularly love the *Lake Queen*, and have an opportunity to actually take the wheel and steer! They might even be named honorary captain!

The *Lake Queen* can be reserved for reunions, wedding parties, anniversaries, and corporate parties. The staff and crew are always obliging, friendly, and eager to help. Breakfast, lunch, and dinner cruises, as well as sightseeing cruises, are available.

For information and reservations write the *Lake Queen*, 280 North Lake Drive, Branson, Missouri 65616, or call (417) 334-3015.

Polynesian Princess

Cruise Table Rock Lake, Polynesian style, aboard the *Polynesian Princess*, a favorite sightseeing and dinner boat. Relaxing and enjoyable breakfast, dinner, or sightseeing cruises tour what many consider to be the most beautiful lake in the Ozarks. While dining, you are treated to magnificent service, great food, and Polynesian entertainment.

The *Polynesian Princess* can be chartered for wedding parties, reunions, private parties, corporate meetings, and even Christmas parties.

For information or reservations call (417) 337-8366 or 1-800-523-7589.

The *Sammy Lane* Pirate Cruise

Billed as "Missouri's oldest continuous attraction," the *Sammy Lane* Boat Line has operated on Lake Taneycomo since 1913. This thrilling seventy-minute cruise offers a number of exciting events one doesn't get to see every day. For one thing, kids can help the captain pilot the boat! For another, you have an opportunity to encounter fierce pirates and actually help save the ship from an attack by these raiders. The *Sammy Lane* also passes by the Boston Ridge Gold Mine and lots of scenic shoreline.

Cruises depart several times each day, and prices are quite reasonable. For information and reservations write to The *Sammy Lane* Pirate Cruise, 280 North Lake Drive, Branson, Missouri 65616, or call (417) 334-3015.

Showboat Branson Belle

A remarkable way to experience Table Rock Lake is aboard the authentic 1890s *Showboat Branson Belle.* Step back in time when these majestic paddle wheelers ruled the rivers and lakes, and enjoy a romantic cruise, fine dining, and a wonderful show.

A guaranteed good time can be found here: You can stroll the decks and enjoy the magnificent sunsets; you can indulge in a wonderful meal from the ship's on-board galley (breakfast, lunch, and dinner); you can party and dance to the music of the great band. Special Christmas and holiday shows are planned every year.

For information and reservations on the breakfast, lunch, and dinner cruises, write to the *Showboat Branson*

Belle, 4800 State Highway 165, Branson, Missouri 65616, or call 1-800-227-8587.

The Ducks!

Ride the Ducks on land, across mountains, and into the lake!

These fun-filled transports, patterned after World War II amphibious vehicles, climb mountains to bring you scenic vistas, move quietly along wooded roads past lush Ozark Mountain scenery, and enter the waters of Table Rock Lake for a relaxing cruise among the stern-wheelers and pleasure boats!

There are two Duck enterprises located in Branson: Ozark Mountain Water Ducks and Ride the Ducks.

Ozark Mountain Water Ducks

Ozark Mountain Water Ducks offer an eighty-minute tour of land and water on a route that winds through the beautiful Ozarks, into Table Rock Lake, and back.

A licensed and U.S. Coast Guard-certified captain, who provides entertaining and historical information about the history of the Ozarks, operates each Duck.

For information call Ozark Mountain Water Ducks at (417) 336-2111.

Ride the Ducks

Adventurous kids are allowed to drive the Ducks and have a chance to earn a captain's certificate. Speaking of the captain, all of the Duck captains are competent, safe, and quite entertaining. Duck riders also receive a free quacker they are encouraged to use during the scenic tour through wooded back roads, up to the top of Baird Mountain, and across Table Rock Lake.

For information write to Ride The Ducks, P.O. Box 1837, Branson, Missouri 65616, or call (417)334-3825.

Helicopter Tours

A unique way to see the fascinating Ozarks and Branson countryside is via helicopter. Remarkably smooth, surprisingly comfortable, and safe, this narrated, informative tour takes travelers over woodland, the town and entertainment center, and beautiful Table Rock Lake.

A helicopter tour is truly not something you get to do every day, and those who have tried it heartily recommend it to others. Spring and fall hours are from 10:00 A.M. to 5:00 P.M. Summer hours are from 9:00 A.M. to 9:00 P.M.

For information call Table Rock Helicopter Tours at (417) 334-6102, or write to them at 3309 West Highway 76, Branson, Missouri 65616.

Hollywood Wax Museum

See lifelike movie stars portrayed in "living wax." Open every day at 8:00 in the morning, the Hollywood Wax Museum takes the visitor on a journey through movie and television history, featuring images of your favorite stars from old movies through today's blockbusters. See remarkably lifelike characters from the Wizard of Oz, and stunningly realistic images of Elvis, Rambo, and many, many more.

For information write to the Hollywood Wax Museum, 3030 76 Country Boulevard, Branson, Missouri 65616, or call (417) 33-STARS.

Ripley's Believe It or Not!

Ripley's Believe It or Not! has long been a favorite feature in the newspapers throughout the world. Today, Ripley's Believe It or Not! Museum of Amazement is now one of the most popular attractions in Branson.

Some of the world's most unbelievable phenomena can be seen and experienced here, including: Liu Ch'ung, a man who has two pupils in each of his eyes; a ball of twine forty-two feet around; a two-headed calf; a replica of an aircraft carrier made from over 48,000 matchsticks. And there is much, much more. Those who have visited Ripley's Believe It or Not! insist it is a must-see and not to leave Branson without a stop here.

Ripley's Believe It or Not! is located in a wacky-looking building that appears to have been cracked open by an earthquake. Ripley's is located on 76 Country Boulevard, one block west of Gretna Road. For more information call (417) 337-5460.

Stone Hill Winery

The Stone Hill Winery began operations in Branson in 1986 but enjoys a history of over 150 years. The winery was originally constructed in the town of Hermann, Missouri, in 1847, and by 1900 was the third largest winery in the world, as well as the second largest in the United States.

In 1920 Prohibition caused the Stone Hill Winery to close. In 1965 Jim and Betty Held purchased the winery and continued the tradition of making fine German wines.

Stone Hill's second winery in Branson has grown to be a rather popular attraction, receiving over 250,000 visitors each year. The tours of the winery are educational and provide some of the history of wine-making in Missouri, as well as explaining how wine is actually made. Following the tour, one can sample a number of these fine wines.

The Stone Hill Winery is open all year long from 8:30 A.M. to dusk. Groups are welcome, and there is plenty of parking on the premises for busses and RVs. For more information write to Stone Hill Winery, 601 State Highway 165, Branson, Missouri 65616, or call (417) 334-1897.

Train Ride!

The Branson Scenic Railway is the only train in town. And what a train it is!

This incredible dinner excursion leaves the downtown Branson depot every Saturday at 5:30 P.M., travels through the scenic countryside, and serves some of the finest dinner entrees you can find anywhere, including prime rib, Pacific red snapper, and butterfly boneless chicken breast. All this, and live entertainment too! The passenger cars are all climate controlled and have modern restrooms.

For information and reservations write to Branson Scenic Railway, 206 East Main Street, Branson, Missouri 65616, or call 1-800-2-TRAIN-2.

White River Bald Natural Area

Located on the Ruth and Paul Henning Conservation Area just west of Branson on Missouri Highway 76 near the Shepherd of the Hills Homestead, this fascinating wildlife treat is nestled on a 362-acre glade replete with hiking trails.

This is a unique and different kind of wildlife area. Here the visitor will see numerous examples of lizards including fence lizards, five-lined skinks, prairie-lined racerunners, collard lizards, and others. Also found here are tarantulas and burrowing scorpions and other fascinating examples of wildlife built low to the ground.

For more information call (417) 334-4865.

Section Eleven

Ozark Caverns

One of the principal characteristics of the limestone and dolomite rock that makes up the bulk of the Ozark Mountains is its suitability for cavern formation. Geologists tell us there are hundreds, perhaps even thousands, of caves honeycombing the Ozark range. Many of them are very tiny, but several are incredibly huge.

During the times when Indians roamed and hunted throughout this region, members of different tribes took shelter in some of these caves. Artifacts from their visits are still being found today by archeologists and hobbyists. When white settlers started moving into the area, some of the early arrivals lived in caves until cabins could be constructed. Caves were also sometimes used to store food and hide valuables, and often served as secret locations of moonshine stills.

A wild cave is defined as one that is not open to commercial use, and hundreds of these sometimes difficult-to-reach caverns exist in the southwestern Missouri and northwestern Arkansas Ozarks. These wild caves offer numerous opportunities for the adventurous spelunker, and organized groups of cavers visit such locations regularly to explore and map.

For the casual tourist, however, a number of commercially developed caves are available, each of them offering grand views of spectacular underground formations and passageways.

Webster's Ninth New Collegiate Dictionary defines a cave as "a natural underground chamber or series of chambers open to the surface." While accurate, that definition simply does not do justice to the beauty and wonder found in many of these caves available to visitors to this part of the Ozarks.

Cavern formation is associated with the process of solution. It is difficult for many people to believe that certain kinds of solid rock can dissolve, but it is true. Limestone and dolomite, sedimentary rocks that make up the bulk of the Ozark Mountains, are among the most soluble. Continued solution, along with the normal weathering and erosion processes, serve to enlarge passageways and chambers.

Environments that produce caverns are also associated with a number of related features. For instance, sinkholes—the collapsed roofs of caves—are common in the Ozarks. Sinking streams and springs, also often associated with caverns, are frequently found in the region.

Among the most appealing features associated with caves are the speleothems, the calcareous deposits composed mainly of calcite. Speleothems include stalactites (the large, icicle-like formations that grow downward from the ceiling of the cave) and stalagmites (the thick, mound-shaped features that grow up from the floor). Occasionally, a stalactite and stalagmite will join together to form a structure called a column.

Another calcareous formation called a drapery originates in a manner similar to stalactites but becomes a wider, flatter, flow-like formation found associated with elongated cracks in the cavern ceilings. Indeed, they look much like the draperies that hang in your home.

There are a number of magnificent caverns found in and within a short drive of Branson. They include:

Blanchard Springs Caverns

Located some eighty miles to the southeast in the Ozark National Forest of Arkansas, this spectacular cavern is well worth a day trip.

This cavern is named after early settler John H. Blanchard, though it is doubtful that Blanchard ever actually saw the cave. Though the cavern was known to most of the local residents, few dared enter the dark and forbidding interior. During the early settlement period, it was called Half-Mile Cave. It wasn't until 1934 that U.S. Forest Service employee Willard Hadley ventured into the cave to explore it. In 1955 the first systematic examination and mapping of the cave took place, an effort that lasted some five years. Blanchard Springs Caverns were finally opened to the public in 1963.

There are at least two levels to this spectacular cavern. The Dripstone Trail takes visitors through the upper level, about three-fourths of a mile's worth of paved pathway with excellent lighting that highlight beautiful calcite formations.

The Discovery Trail takes visitors on an excursion through the lower level, a far more exhausting walk and not recommended for the infirm or out-of-shape.

Located in a beautiful part of the Ozarks and adjacent to camping and picnicking facilities, Blanchard Springs Caverns is open year round and is one of the jewels in the Ozark Mountain cavern system.

For information call (870) 757-2211.

Bluff Dwellers Cave

Located about one hour west of Branson near the town of Noel, Missouri, is Bluff Dwellers Cave.

Bluff Dwellers Cave takes its name from the numerous artifacts and human bones found nearby while it was being readied for commercial visitation.

Missourian C.A. Browning first explored Bluff Dwellers Cave in 1925 and opened it to the public in 1927. Though the cavern is not particularly large, it offers a number of interesting and picturesque formations of dripstone, stalactites, draperies, and soda straws.

For information call (417) 475-3666.

Bull Shoals Caverns

Located right next to the tiny Arkansas town of Bull Shoals on Arkansas Highway 178, this unique cave was home to Indians and early settlers alike because of its continuous supply of fresh water. Inside this cave, one finds a stream (with trout!), a lake, and an impressive waterfall.

Bull Shoals Caverns is open March through November. The town of Bull Shoals provides adequate lodging, restaurants, and other services. Camping is easily found on the shores of Bull Shoals Lake.

For information call (870) 445-2101.

Civil War Cave

Located near Bentonville, some fifty miles southwest of Branson, this comparatively small cave possesses an interesting history. During the Civil War, the underground stream found within provided fresh water for Confederate troops who camped nearby. Reportedly, the soldiers used the cave's interior to store ammunition and supplies. In addition to the underground stream, the inside of the cave features a lake and a number of small, attractive pools of water formed by calcareous rimstone dams.

Civil War Cave is open throughout the year except for the winter months. The tour through the cavern takes only half an hour. Associated with the site are a gift shop along with camping and picnicking facilities.

For information write Route 3, Box 84, Bentonville, Arkansas 72712.

Cosmic Caverns

Cosmic Caverns, located about thirty miles southwest of Branson and not far from the Arkansas town of Berryville, was discovered by area residents around the beginning of the Civil War. This impressive cavern was once featured on *CBS News* during the early 1990s.

Deep within the cave are two lakes. Lotus Lake is believed to be the largest underground lake of any cave found in the Ozarks. South Lake is called "bottomless." Blind cave trout have been seen swimming in South Lake.

In addition to the lakes, one of the most attractive features is a pure white onyx flowstone formation called The Frozen Milky Way. In a recently opened section of the cave, pure white soda straw and helictite formations greet visitors. The new area is so pristine, many of the formations are transparent.

Onyx was found in Cosmic Caverns during the early 1900s, and for a ten-year period was heavily mined and shipped to nearby Eureka Springs where it was fashioned into doorknobs.

Cosmic Caverns is open during the entire year, and the log visitor center features tourist information, a rock shop, gift shop, and a fudge kitchen.

For information call (870) 749-2298.

Crystal Cave

Crystal Cave, though an enjoyable tour, has intentionally not been developed quite as much as most of the other caves in this part of the Ozarks and offers visitors a look at what a natural cave can be like. Lighting and facilities are kept to a minimum, and the purpose of this is to provide the visitor with a feeling of entering and exploring a cave under the most natural conditions possible.

For its size, Crystal Cave offers an impressive variety of underground formations, including dripstone, stalactites, stalagmites, and draperies. Well worth a visit, Crystal Cave is open May through December.

For information call (501) 883-0031.

Crystal Caverns

Crystal Caverns (not be confused with Crystal Cave above) are located near the town of Cassville, Missouri, about thirty miles west of Branson.

The cave was discovered in 1854 when a sinkhole suddenly collapsed and revealed a sophisticated cave system several dozen feet below the surface. While occasionally explored over the next seventy years, it was not opened to commercial traffic until 1938.

Within the passageways and chambers of Crystal Caverns can be seen a wide variety of formations, the most unusual of which is regarded to be the black stalactites! Black stalactites are considered to be quite rare.

The tour through the cave covers only one-half mile and takes approximately forty-five minutes. The caverns are open March through November.

For information call (417) 849-4238.

Devils Den Cave

Located about eighty miles southwest of Branson in Arkansas' beautiful Devils Den State Park, this cave, according to local history, was a hiding place for area outlaws, as well as bands of horse thieves that ranged throughout Oklahoma and western Arkansas. The region was extremely isolated 100 years ago.

The outlaws were eventually run out of the area, and by the mid-1930s the Civilian Conservation Corps constructed roads into the area that is now the park.

The Devils Den Cave tour is short, yet impressive. Self-guided, the last half of the walk is quite difficult for the inexperienced. Visitors, who must bring their own flashlights, are warned to exercise caution.

For information call (501) 761-3325.

Diamond Cave

Located near Jasper, Arkansas, an easy and quite scenic one-hour drive south from Branson, Diamond Cave makes for a pleasurable day trip.

There are no diamonds in Diamond Cave, but this interesting cavern does offer a number of impressive formations. Cave operators and local residents like to relate the story of a visit to the cave by early explorer Frederick Gerstaker. While hunting for bear one afternoon, Gerstaker and his partner followed an adult black bear to the mouth of the cave. Sending their dogs into the cavern after the animal, the two men then fashioned some crude torches and followed. Moments later they heard the sounds of a fight between the bear and the dogs. The end result was that all of the dogs were killed. About 200 feet into the cave, the bear attacked Gerstaker and his companion, severely injuring them both. Before the fight was over, however, the intrepid hunters finally killed the bear.

Diamond Cave is open throughout the entire year save for the winter months. For information call (870) 446-2636.

Fantastic Caverns

Fantastic Caverns are located about an hour's drive north of Branson and just a few short miles northwest of Springfield. Visitors to this cave can observe the entire length of it via a ride in a jeep-drawn tram through the passageways in year-round sixty degree temperature, even when the outdoor temperature drops below freezing or rises above 100 degrees. The cavern's auditorium is sometimes the site of entertainment ranging from bluegrass to symphonic music.

Fantastic Caverns are open year round, and the short tour takes only half an hour. Camping and picnicking facilities are located nearby. For more information call (417) 883-2010.

Honey Branch Cave

Honey Branch Cave is located about one hour northeast of Branson near the town of Ava. Area Indians long used this cave as a shelter during hunting expeditions into the once-remote Ozark Mountains. A number of artifacts found in and adjacent to the cave have supported the notion that it was used as late as the 1880s.

From time to time since 1956, Honey Branch Cave has been opened for tours. These days, it is open year round, and it takes approximately forty-five minutes to an hour to enjoy the guided tour. For information call (417) 683-0269.

Hurricane River Cave

Located about forty miles south of Branson near the small community of Elkhead, Hurricane River Cave, also called Hurricane Cave and Big Hurricane Cave, has delighted visitors for years.

Hurricane River Cave features a forty-five-minute guided tour during which the visitor can observe some impressive cave formations including draperies, stalactites, and stalagmites.

The cave was once occupied by Indians and early settlers and derives its name from its continued use as a shelter during severe storms that struck this area.

Hurricane River Cave is open all year long. For information call (870) 439-2343.

Marvel Cave

Marvel Cave was once called Marble Cave and is located on the grounds of the Silver Dollar City theme park. Marvel Cave contains over twenty different passageways and three separate underground streams.

William Lynch first explored Marvel Cave during the 1880s. For a time, huge deposits of bat guano were mined from the cave and sold as fertilizer. In 1891 Lynch purchased the property on which the cave was located and spent most of the rest of his life exploring and developing it. In 1894 Lynch opened the cave to the public.

Originally, Lynch called the cavern Marble Cave, because he mistakenly identified some of the cavern rock as marble.

Inside Marvel Cave, the visitor is entranced by a twenty-story high room that can be entered only through the ceiling! Some five hundred feet underground, one can observe an impressive waterfall.

Marvel Cave is open to the public March through December. A gift shop, food, and arts and crafts are available nearby. For more information call (417) 338-2611.

Old Spanish Treasure Cave

Located about seventy-five miles southwest of Branson near the town of Sulphur Springs, Arkansas, this cave is the source of a fascinating legend of lost Spanish treasure believed by many to have been buried here (see Section Five, Folklore). Efforts to locate the treasure have been thwarted by cave-ins and flooding. The cave is filled with a number of confusing passageways resembling a maze.

For information call (501) 787-5155.

Onyx Cave

Onyx Cave is located approximately four miles east of Eureka Springs, Arkansas, and only about thirty-five miles southwest of Branson. While Onyx Cave has been a commercial attraction in this area since 1910, it is perhaps most famous for the special and rare clay found within. Potters prize the Onyx Cave clay and have mined it for several years.

Onyx Cave is open throughout the year. It offers a fascinating self-guided tour with some sophisticated lighting effects and features some impressively large, translucent formations.

A museum is located on the premises and is free to visitors.

Ozark Wonder Cave

Located near the town of Noel and only a few minutes from Bluff Dwellers Cave, Ozark Wonder Cave features fascinating displays of stalactites, stalagmites, draperies, columns, and domes.

The cave was reputedly discovered in 1862 by Confederate soldiers assigned to General Sterling Price's regiment. Opened to the public in 1915 by a man named Truit, Ozark Wonder Cave has become a tourist favorite.

For more information call (417) 475-3579.

Talking Rocks Cave

Located in Reeds Springs, just a few minutes northwest of Branson, Talking Rocks Cave was called Fairy Cave until recent years. First discovered in 1883, this cavern was not thoroughly explored until 1896 when Truman Powell entered it. Powell, incidentally, was the model for the shepherd in Harold Bell Wright's play *The Shepherd of the Hills*.

For several years, Powell and his family maintained the cave as a tourist attraction before finally selling it to the Silver Dollar City theme park.

Talking Rocks Cave is regarded by many speleologists as one of the most interesting and picturesque of the Ozark caverns, offering thousands of some of the most elaborate formations of flowstone and draperies found anywhere. Above the cavern is a four-hundred-acre nature preserve including a number of hiking trails and spectacular views of the Ozark hills.

Talking Rocks Cavern serves as a sanctuary for the rare Ozark Blind Cave Salamander. Occasionally, one or more of these endangered species is spotted during a tour of the cave.

Talking Rocks Cave is open daily throughout the year and has become a popular destination for Branson visitors. For information call 1 (800) 600-CAVE.

War Eagle Cave

War Eagle Cave is located east of Rogers, Arkansas, on State Highway 12. At this writing, the cave is still being explored and mapped, with about ten miles completed thus far. The portion of the cave that is open to the public offers impressive displays of draperies, rimstone, stalactites, and stalagmites.

War Eagle Cave is open May though December. For information call (501) 789-2909.

Civil War Battlefield Sites

Within a short drive from Branson can be found three historically important Civil War battlefield sites.

The southwestern Missouri and northwestern Arkansas Ozarks lacked any kind of significant population during the War Between the States, and the region boasted few, if any, resources or strategic locations important to either the Union or Confederate army. In spite of its unlikely potential for serving as a setting for major military engagements, this general region, along with nearby northwestern Arkansas, is the location of a trio of major battles: the Battle of Pea Ridge, the Battle of Prairie Grove, and the Battle of Wilson's Creek.

The Battle of Wilson's Creek

Wilson's Creek National Battlefield is located ten miles southwest of downtown Springfield, less than an hour's drive from Branson.

The Battle of Wilson's Creek, which took place on August 10, 1861, has been called by historians the most important Civil War confrontation fought west of the Mississippi River. General Nathaniel Lyon led his Union troops numbering 4,000 against a General Sterling Price-led Confederate force in excess of 10,000 men.

When Lyon learned the Confederate army was camped at Wilson's Creek, he decided to launch an attack, hoping the element of surprise would offset the overwhelming odds.

It didn't.

The battle, one of the most bloody in the annals of Civil War history, left over 2,300 dead men on the field, including Lyon himself. Though the Rebels were victorious, the loss of men weakened their efforts to maintain a secure foothold in the Ozark Mountains.

The visitors' center at Wilson's Creek National Battlefield features a museum, a film, and a map of the battlefield. A hiking and biking trail winds through the park, and visitors can indulge in a self-guided auto-tour of a portion of the battlefield along a paved road. For information call (417) 732-2662.

The Battle of Pea Ridge

The site of the Battle of Pea Ridge is now a national military park and is located about forty-five miles westsouthwest of Branson and just across the border in Arkansas. Easy access to the park is via scenic Arkansas Highway 62. While the Federals labeled this bloody encounter as the Battle of Pea Ridge, the Confederates always refer to it as the Battle of Elkhorn Tavern.

The battle took place March 6-8, 1862, and has been described by historians as a major victory for the Union forces. The Union soldiers, led by General Samuel R. Curtis, engaged a General Earl Van Dorn-led Confederate force.

The Confederates outnumbered the Yankees two to one, and among the Rebel ranks were over one thousand American Indians, including Cherokees, Choctaws, Chicasaws, Creeks, and Seminoles. The Indian contingent was led by General Albert Pike and, in part, by the famous Cherokee leader Stand Watie.

In spite of lacking adequate food, supplies, clothing, ammunition, and experienced staff, Van Dorn attempted to get behind Curtis's smaller army and cut off retreat. To further complicate plans, a blizzard struck the region just as Van Dorn's troops got under way. Curtis, anticipating Van Dorn's action, pulled his force into a strong defensive position along Little Sugar Creek and merely waited.

The three-day battle was violent and bloody, and by the time it was over, the Confederates were soundly defeated. Two important Confederate generals—Ben McCulloch, who fell early in the fighting, and James I. McIntosh, who followed shortly thereafter—were killed during the confrontation. A third general—W.Y. Slack— was rendered ineffective as a result of a mortal wound.

Having lost their leaders, the Confederates were confused and disorganized. As it became clear the Federals would be victorious, the Rebels fled from the region, traveling southward toward the Arkansas River. At first, Union General Sterling Price wanted to pursue the fleeing enemy, but he eventually reconsidered.

In all, the Confederates reported over 2,000 soldiers killed or wounded. Union losses totaled 1,384.

The Yankee victory at Pea Ridge is noteworthy for two things: So compelling was the dominance over the Confederates that the South never regained complete control of this part of the Ozarks, or even expressed much interest in retaking the region. Secondly, the Indians, who entered the fray with concerns and confusion over allegiance, ultimately aligned themselves with the North.

The Battle of Pea Ridge, where the Confederates were soundly defeated, has been called "The Gettysburg of the West."

The Battle of Prairie Grove

Prairie Grove, Arkansas, is located about eighty miles southwest of Branson in Washington Country. Easily reached via Arkansas Highway 62, this attractive state park is visited by thousands each year.

The town of Prairie Grove has a population of a bit less than 2,000 friendly souls, a quiet main street, and is surrounded by gently rolling, peaceful countryside. Driving through the area, it is difficult to believe that a bitter battle between Union and Confederate forces was fought here during the winter of 1862.

After assembling a Confederate force of 9,000 infantrymen and 2,300 cavalrymen, along with twenty-two canons, at Van Buren, Arkansas, General Thomas C. Hindman led them through the snow and cold into the Ozark Mountains. Hindman's intention was to engage and defeat a Union force of 7,000 men led by General James G. Blunt.

Hindman initially planned to catch up to Blunt's army at Cane Hill, six miles southwest of Prairie Grove. Blunt, on learning that Hindman's army was approaching, requested aid from General Francis J. Herron at Yellville, Arkansas. After quickly organizing his troops, Herron left Yellville and arrived at Fayetteville just as the Confederates launched their attack.

Hindman intended to wedge his forces in between Blunt's army and the oncoming Herron. Hindman believed if he could keep the two Union forces from uniting, then victory over both of them would be a cinch.

Although the Rebels successfully intercepted Herron's advance, the ill-prepared infantry was unable to capitalize on the strategy. Instead, Hindman ordered his army to retreat to a position at Prairie Grove where he took up a defensive position to await the Federals.

With Hindman's retreat to Prairie Grove, Blunt moved quickly to join with Herron. As this occurred, Herron directed a portion of his forces to attack Hindman on December 7, 1862. The fierce battle raged back and forth across the hills and valleys and even into a nearby orchard and cornfield. For a time, it appeared as though the Confederates were going to defeat Herron, but a large contingent of troops led by Blunt flanked the Rebels.

By sunset, the battlefield was littered with the dead— 1,317 Confederates and 1,251 Union soldiers. Realizing his soldiers were low on ammunition and supplies and fearful of additional Yankee reinforcements, Hindman flew a white flag under the pretense of collecting his wounded troops from the battlefield. As this took place, Hindman, gathering most of his men together, escaped to the south.

As the Confederates fled, Blunt followed their route into Van Buren on the banks of the Arkansas River where he conducted a raid and captured weapons and food.

At Prairie Grove, the South suffered defeat at the hands of the Union army once again and never attempted to enter the area again as an avenue of invasion into Missouri.

Prairie Grove Battlefield State Park, which includes 306 acres of the 3,000-acre battlefield offers a museum, audiovisual programs, musket demonstrations, and other educational activities. Guided tours are scheduled daily.

Section Thirteen

Shopping

A recent newspaper article referred to Branson, Missouri, as "America's Fastest Growing Shopping Mecca." In this town of only 4,000 permanent residents, but with millions of visitors each year, hundreds of name-brand factory outlet stores, as well as unique, independently owned retail shops, await the traveler. In fact, a recent survey named Branson as the Number Three major outlet shopping destination in America. New stores are opening almost daily, and ground is constantly being broken to accommodate new shopping locations.

Mall and Outlet Shopping

Branson Mall

It seems like everybody who visits Branson comes to the Branson Mall at one time or another. This fine mall has a little bit of everything, including entertainment, coffee shops, and music stores.

The shops here include Consumers, the Ernest Tubb Record Shop, a wig shop, and even a Wal-Mart. Located at 2206 76 Country Boulevard, Branson Mall is convenient to downtown. For more information call (417) 334-5412.

Engler Block

"A Unique Shopping Mall," says the sign. And it's true. Here, the visitor can actually watch craftsmen make many of the products sold here. Located two blocks east of the Dixie Stampede, the Engler Block features an old-time photo studio, art studios, Cappuccino Country, a woodcarver, Father Time Clocks and Collectibles, Glass Magic, Golden Images, Mastercraft Puppets, The Pottery Shop, Sunrise Leatherworks, and many more. In addition, the hungry shopper can dine at Cobbler and Sandwich Shoppe, The Fudgery, or Steak and Berries Restaurant.

The Engler Block is located at 1335 76 Country Boulevard. For information call (417) 335-2200.

Factory Merchants Branson

This large, red-roofed mall houses over ninety bargain-filled outlets along with six fine restaurants. Located on Pat Nash Road just off West Highway 76, Factory Merchants Branson is easy to drive to and convenient to the rest of the town. Here, the shopper can find a wide selection of children's, men's, and women's fashions, jewelry, cosmetics, home furnishings, luggage, leather, shoes, kitchen accessories, and much, much more, all with advertised savings of from twenty-five to seventy-five percent off ticketed prices.

For information call (417) 335-6686.

Factory Shoppes

Factory Shoppes advertises "Factory Direct Savings of Up to 70% on All Your Favorite Brand Names." If you like outlet shopping, this might be just the place for you. At Factory Shoppes, the visitor will find thirty stores carrying men's, women's, and children's fashions, home accessories, books, footwear, and more. Shops including Bugle Boy, Duck Head, Bostonian Shoe, Mountain Man Nut and Fruit, Easy Spirit, Big and Tall Casual Male,

Paper Factory, T-Shirts Plus, Farberware, Totes, Sunglasses World, Spiegel Outlet Store, and more.

On the premises are two favorite places to eat: Jimmy's Restaurant and the Years Gone By Coffee and Dessert Shop.

Factory Shoppes is located at Branson Meadows at Roark Valley Road and Gretna Road and is open from 9:00 A.M. to 9:00 P.M. Monday through Saturday, and 9:00 A.M. to 7:00 P.M. on Sunday. For more information call 1-800-SHOP-USA.

Grand Village

Conveniently located near the Grand Palace and at the center of the entertainment section of Branson, the Grand Village features twenty-six one-of-a-kind shops and two fine eateries—the Hard Luck Diner and the Village Cafe—in a quaint cobblestone village setting. Here you can find gifts, souvenirs, collectibles, home accents, books, and lots more. Shops include Remember When, Classic Collectibles, Bear Hollow, Jimmie Dee's Fine Metals, The Ivy Gate, Katherine's Jewelry, Ozark Mountain

Entrance to Grand Village Shopping Mall

Grand Village Shopping Mall is clean and spacious.

Gifts, Grandma's Baby Dolls, T. Charleston and Sons Bookstore, and others.

The Grand Village has ample parking and is within easy walking distance of several motels, restaurants, and shows. For more information call (417) 336-SHOP.

Tanger Outlet Center

The Tanger Outlet folks claim the average customer saves forty percent off retail prices here every day. This outlet mall is home to sixty brand name manufacturers, including Bass, Fossil, Haggar Clothing Company, Liz Claiborne, Maidenform, Oshkosh B'Gosh, Reebok, Stone Mountain Handbags, Tommy Hilfiger, and many, many more.

Tanger Outlet Center is located at 300 Tanger Boulevard. For information call (417) 337-9327.

Victorian Village Shops

With over twenty distinctively different stores, the folks at Victorian Village Shops advertise that this is "Where we take shopping personally." Claiming a vast variety of versatile shops and shows, this attractive complex also houses the Braschler Village Theater, as well as a number of stores including Arkansas Diamond, Ballenger's, Bear Necessities, Branson Hotline, Branson Music, Cappuccino Country, Gingerbread Kids, Heart to Heart, Heavenly Happenings, Leather Etc., Mirror's Image, Mulberry Mill, Post Net, Silver Highlights, Southwest Gifts, Sweet Dreams, and White River Trading Company.

Victorian Village Shops is easy to reach at 3044 Shepherd of the Hills Expressway. For more information call (417) 334-4363.

VF Factory Outlet

VF Factory Outlet touts price, quality, service, and satisfaction as its greatest assets. At VF, which is the anchor store at the Factory Stores of America Outlet Center, you purchase direct from the manufacturer with no middleman, therefore saving 1/2 off the lowest ticketed price. Quality translates into name brands, which fill these stores. VF also takes pride in their friendly and helpful salespeople. Satisfaction is guaranteed: If the purchaser is not satisfied with an item, he or she may return it for refund or exchange, no questions asked.

VF Factory claims the largest selections of jeans, lingerie, and sweat suits in the area. In Branson, they can be found at 4340 Gretna Road, just a few minutes from downtown. For more information call (417) 339-4812.

Strip Malls

Lots of clean, busy strip malls can be found in Branson, all of them containing unique shops, great bargains, and even some fine restaurants.

The Falls Center

Located near the Tony Orlando Theater, the Falls Center is a pleasant little strip mall with several fine specialty shops including Golf USA, a jewelry store, Dressin' Gaudy, a western wear store, and several more.

In addition, there are two nice restaurants located in the Falls Center—McGuffey's and St. Louis Bread Company.

For more information call (417) 334-3400.

The Market Place

Branson visitors who stay at the Welk Resort are familiar with The Market Place, for this nifty little strip mall is located right next door. Several one-of-a-kind shops can be found here, including Dolly Dears, which some say is the largest seller of dolls in the United States; Old West, a hip art gallery with an ice cream parlor; and Lasting Interiors for home furnishings and accessories.

Visitors often report spotting big name entertainers shopping at The Market Place. For more information call (417) 366-2468.

IMAX Center

A lot of people think the IMAX is a big movie house. That's true, but associated with this fine facility are a number of shops well worth the time it takes to drive out here.

At the IMAX Center, you will find Bekemeier's Apple Butter Shoppe, featuring batch cooking of some delightful apple butter as well as other flavors such as peach, blackberry, and apricot butters.

At the IMAX, one will also find The Trading Post, an American Indian arts and crafts store with everything from postcards to jewelry.

For more information call (417) 335-4832.

Historic Downtown Branson

Other than the fact that it is more crowded with visitors, downtown Branson looks much the same today as it did fifty years ago. Only a few square blocks in size, the downtown area can be browsed and shopped easily and without a lot of walking.

Aux-Arcs Cross Stitcher's Heaven

Aux Arcs is the original French way of saying Ozarks. The Aux-Arcs Cross Stitcher's Heaven is a fascinating little store that features some of the finest in needlework supplies, patterns, threads, and fabrics. The needlework hobbyist can't pass up this friendly store. If you have a friend who does needlework, this is the place to come for gifts.

The Aux-Arcs is located at 224 West Main. For more information call (417) 334-5278.

Branson Mercantile and Company

Branson Mercantile is the town's oldest clothier (est. 1945) and features three floors of quality brand name merchandise. This is the place where locals come to purchase their jeans and shirts.

The Branson Mercantile and Company is located at 120 South Commercial Street. For more information call (417) 334-3634.

Brier Rose and Ivy Rose Quilts and Gifts

A lot of people travel to the Ozarks with the expectation of finding locally made, hand-crafted quilts. One of the best places to do so, we are told, is the Brier Rose. This place has one of the largest selections of "made in the Ozarks" quilts you can find. Prices on these fine quilts range from bargain level upward to several thousand dollars. But don't stop at the quilts—the Brier Rose stocks a lot of other interesting crafts.

Brier Rose is located at 117 East Main Street. For more information call (417) 336-3436.

Dick's Oldtime 5 & 10

You will find a lot of things in Dick's Oldtime 5 & 10 you won't find in other stores. For instance, here you can look over a fascinating arrowhead collection, an old player piano, and over fifty signed World War II aviation prints. This old-time variety store carries over 50,000 items.

Sometimes, Dick's Oldtime 5 & 10 has the feel of a museum more than of a retail store, but that just makes it all the more fun.

Dick's is located at 103 West Main. For information call (417) 334-2410

The Doll Depot

The name says it all. Dolls, dolls, and more dolls. A large percentage of the dolls found in this tidy little shop are made by local craftspersons.

The Doll Depot is located at 112 South Commercial Street. For more information call (417) 335-4438.

The Fudge Shop

Homemade fudge and other goodies fill the display case at The Fudge Shop. And not just chocolate flavored fudge, either. Here, you can find lots of fudge flavors including vanilla, walnut, peanut butter, and others.

A nice feature offered by The Fudge Shop is a mailing service. You can place an order and they will mail it to wherever you want. This is a great way to handle Christmas and other gifts.

The Fudge Shop is located on Business Highway 65. For information call (417) 334-5270.

If The Shoe Fits

This store sells quality women's shoes, and they carry lots of hard-to-find sizes and widths. Some great bargains can be found here. If The Shoe Fits is located at 104 South Commercial. For more information call (417) 334-6740.

Kendall Company Christmas and Toys

At the Kendall Company, it is Christmas all year long. A vast collection of Christmas decorations, toys, and gifts can be found here, and it's not uncommon to find a lot of Christmas shopping going on during the summer here.

Kendall Company Christmas and Toys is located at 109 South Commercial. For more information call (417) 337-8111.

Main Street Jewelry and Gifts

This store has been around for half a century and offers quality and stylishly beautiful gold and diamond jewelry, silver, and crystal. A wide and varied assortment of items can be found here, ranging from paperweights to pewter to some of the most attractive jewelry in the region.

Main Street Jewelry and Gifts is located at 109A Main Street in downtown Branson. For more information call (417) 335-4390.

Mountain Man of the Ozarks Mercantile

In spite of the long and interesting name for this store, it is a gift shop specializing, in part, in candies, fruits, and nuts. It's fun to browse, sample some of the free goodies, and stock up on gifts for friends and relatives.

Mountain Man of the Ozarks Mercantile is located at 118 East Main Street. For information call 1-800-336-6203.

Mountain Music Shop

This dandy music shop offers a wide selection of instruments, new and used, including guitars, banjos, fiddles, mandolins, dulcimers, and more. Strings, picks, capos, and other musical accessories are available. The friendly staff will help you with your selections and will even show you how to play a dulcimer for free!

Mountain Music Shop is located on Business Highway 65. For information call (417) 334-0515.

Mountain Music Shop in downtown Branson

Patricia's House Victorian Gifts

Victorian style is found throughout the town of Branson—in the architecture, in some of the hotels and motels, and in a lot of living and dining rooms. If Victorian decorating is your style, everything you will need can be found here. The helpful staff will even help you with your designs.

Patricia's House is located at 101 West Main Street. For information call (417) 335-4438.

Sugar Shack

The Sugar Shack is much, much more than it appears to be at first look. This fine store carries lots of cooking accessories and cookbooks. Sure, you can find sugary things to satisfy your sweet tooth, but don't neglect the delicious herbs and spices sold in bulk at considerable savings. If you need to take a break, the word around town is that the espresso bar in the back of the store is good place for lunch.

The Sugar Shack is located at 203 South Commercial Street. For more information call (417) 335-8237.

Great Places To Dine: Restaurants, Cafes, Bistros, and Taverns

For years, Branson was known as a great place to go for a weekend fishing trip. Visitors from around the country came to this once sleepy Ozark town to catch bass and panfish, revel in the dynamic scenery, and let the family get in some hiking and horseback riding.

During the 1970s, Branson became known as a kind of entertainment capital for the American Midwest, and soon people were arriving in greater numbers than ever to attend the spectacular performances and other events that go on all day long.

During the boom times of the seventies and eighties, the numbers of entertainers and visitors alike needed places to eat, drink, and in general hang out with one another. As a result, along with the proliferation of showplaces, shopping malls, and fishing camps, Branson now boasts a number of impressive restaurants and bars where folks gather to have fun and enjoy one another.

Applebee's Neighborhood Bar and Grill

Although Applebee's features complete brunch, lunch, and dinner menus, it is best known for its delicious salads and desserts. In recent months, Applebee's has become a favored hangout for after-show gatherings of Branson visitors, musicians, and occasionally a headline performer or two. Try the weekend brunch after a morning of sleeping late from the previous night's activities.

Applebee's, 1836 76 Country Boulevard. 336-5053.

B.T. Bones Steakhouse

Open seven days a week for lunch and dinner. Daily lunch specials are available, but returning diners always seem to go for the steak sandwich. Dinners feature chicken, seafood, and, some say, the best prime rib in Branson, as well as some incredibly delicious steaks. The one-half-pound Texas burgers, along with some of the fine appetizers, make for a great lunch. There is also a vegetarian menu. You'll find entertainment nightly at B.T. Bones, featuring recording artists Joni Carter and Carl Bird. Dancing, cocktails, and no cover charge!

B.T. Bones is open from 11:00 A.M. until past midnight Monday through Saturday.

B.T. Bones Steakhouse, 2280 Shepherd of the Hills Expressway. 335-2002.

Baldknobbers Country Restaurant

An established restaurant featuring breakfast, lunch, and dinner. The dinner buffet attracts lots of folks before the evening shows, so get there early. Service is great, staff is friendly, and the food is tasty.

Baldknobbers Country Restaurant, 2843 76 Country Boulevard. 334-7202.

Banjo's Eatery and Sports Pub

Only about a three-minute drive south of Branson one finds the peaceful little burg of Hollister. Some who wish to escape the hustle and bustle of Branson often take the short drive to Hollister to sample the fare at several excellent eateries in that little town.

A number of regulars can be found at Banjo's on any given day—they come for the camaraderie, the pool tables, and, most of all, for the food. Particularly appealing at Banjo's are the weekday specials such as chicken-fried steak and meatloaf. Salads and sandwiches are great here, as are some of the esoteric menu items such as pork rinds. Everything is quite affordable, and Banjo's is always just plain fun.

Banjo's is located a couple of miles south of Branson in Hollister at 24 Downing Street. 334-4142.

Barker's Branding Iron

Shades of West Texas! Barker's Branding Iron offers a free sixty-four-ounce sirloin—free, that is, if you can consume it, along with vegetables, toast, and drink, at one sitting. Not many can accomplish this feat, but it is fun trying. It is probably more fun watching others try!

In addition to this wonderful dinner come-on, Barker's, best described as a family restaurant, serves up some truly fine steaks as well as a dandy breakfast.

Barker's Branding Iron, 1211 76 Country Boulevard, Branson. 335-4143.

The Bearded Clam

The short drive from Branson to Kimberling City is well worth the time it takes to enjoy a meal at The Bearded Clam. Particularly appealing is dining out on the deck where you can enjoy a view of picturesque Table

Rock Lake as you indulge in the pleasures of the fine steaks and quality seafood served here. Speaking of seafood, The Bearded Clam serves up fresh clams, as well as oysters on the half-shell. If you don't have time to eat here, they have carry-out.

On Friday and Saturday nights, The Bearded Clam has live entertainment.

The Bearded Clam, Highway 13, Kimberling City. 739-4440.

Belgian Waffle and Pancake House

This breakfast and lunch place features a varied menu, cooked-to-order breakfasts, and fresh bakery goods. As might be expected, waffles are a big hit here, and the French toast, everyone tells us, is also quite good.

Lunch consists of blue-plate specials, delicious sandwiches and fresh salads. A number of low-fat entrees are also available.

The Belgian Waffle and Pancake House is located one-half block west of Presleys' Theater. 334-8484.

Beverly's Steakhouse and Saloon

Just ask any longtime Branson resident where to go to have a nice quiet meal of great steak, and they will likely tell you to head down the highway to Beverly's Steakhouse and Saloon. They can tell you exactly how to get there because that is exactly where many of them go themselves for a quiet lunch and a delicious dinner.

Low overhead and nothing fancy, but if you want top-notch steaks, prime rib, fried chicken, or shrimp, this is the place to go.

Beverly's Steakhouse and Saloon, 2449 Missouri Highway 248. 334-6508. Open Monday through Saturday, lunch and dinner. No credit cards.

Branson Cafe

The oldest cafe in town, the Branson Cafe boasts about the "real home cookin'." This is no idle boast. The Branson Cafe is open for breakfast, lunch, and dinner. This is the place to go for exposure to the locals and to some fine dining fare. This is a down-home restaurant with friendly waitresses, excellent food, generous portions, and shockingly low prices. The Branson Cafe opens Monday through Saturday a 5:30 A.M.

Branson Cafe, 120 West Main Street. 334-3021.

Brass Apple Restaurant

A new restaurant featuring a bakery, gourmet coffee shop, a gift shop, and catering. Opens daily at 7:00 A.M. Features live music and dancing.

Brass Apple Restaurant, 405 South Highway 165. 339-3255.

Buckingham's

Walking into Buckingham's (located in the Palace Inn) is like walking into a cross between a museum and Graceland. Wildlife images and skins adorn the place, and palm trees are scattered throughout, lending kind of an African-expedition ambience to the place.

Not only are the decorations unusual, the menu contains some surprises also. Among the standard dishes, one can find smoked ostrich (expensive but truly excellent!), smoked trout, shrimp Newburg, and all kinds of fresh seafood entrees. Whatever you order for dinner, by all means save some room for the incredible desserts. If you don't, you will regret it. I have never been able to leave Buckingham's without experiencing what some claim is the best bread pudding, not just in Branson, but in the world! Quite a claim, indeed, but one which is accepted by many of us who have tried it.

Buckingham's is a dinner choice for honeymooners, and private dining areas enclosed by curtains are available. The wine list may be the most impressive in town.

Buckingham's serves only dinner and a Sunday brunch. Buckingham's is located at 2820 76 Country Boulevard. 337-7777.

Candlestick

The Candlestick, located on the low prominence called Mount Branson just across Lake Taneycomo from the old downtown area, has long been a favored gathering place for area writers, musicians, performers, and just plain folks. The bar and restaurant, which overlook the lake and the town, are neat, clean, and quiet, and are staffed by competent waiters and bartenders.

A lot of business executives bring their clients to the Candlestick for dinner and feed them the exquisite prime rib, oysters, crab, and other seafood, much of which is flown in on a daily basis.

Because of the local popularity of this excellent restaurant, it is always a good idea to make reservations for dinner, the only meal served here. Should the dining room be filled, however, meals can also be served in the comfortable and friendly bar.

Candlestick is located on Candlestick Road, just a short distance east of Branson on Highway 76. 334-3633.

Champagne's

A type of food that is growing in popularity throughout the country these days is Cajun style, and Cajun

restaurants are proliferating throughout the contermi-
nous United States at a great rate. Branson is no
exception, and this town is fortunate to have Champagne's serving up some of the finest gumbo, jambalaya, and
crawfish this side of the Louisiana bayous.

Owned and operated by a real Cajun (Bob Champagne), Champagne's Cajun food is darned tasty, filling,
and reasonably priced.

Champagne's, 2206 76 Country Boulevard, Branson.
334-6410. Open seven days a week serving lunch and
dinner.

Cielito Lindo

Cielito Lindo offers Tex-Mex fare that is acceptable to
a variety of tastes and experiences. The visitor who has
never experienced Tex-Mex food in any form or fashion
will not hurt themselves here—moderate seasoning
allows the food to be enjoyed by young and old alike.

Cielito Lindo, 3515 76 Country Boulevard, Branson.
336-4451. Open seven days a week.

Contrary Mary's

Contrary Mary's is a good place to dine just before or
just after watching a show at the Shoji Tabuchi Theater,
which is only a few steps away. Word of mouth has it that
the old-fashioned chicken and dressing is the most popular selection on the buffet, although a locally famous
writer claims the catfish is the best he's ever had anywhere.

Contrary Mary's, 3292 Shepherd of the Hills Expressway. 334-7700.

Cowboy Cafe

This is what the Hard Rock Cafe would look like if it went country and western! Gold records, clothes, and musical instruments hang from the walls, inviting customers to look, read, and admire.

There is more than glitz at the Cowboy Cafe, however, for the food served up at lunch and dinner is plentiful and good. The buffet attracts many, but the fine menu is also filled with some exciting dishes.

Cowboy Cafe is located at 526 Shepherd of the Hills Expressway. 335-4828.

Desert Cafe

A spacious, friendly restaurant serving all of your favorite Mexican dishes and more. Great appetizers, great entrees, even some darned good barbecue and steaks.

Desert Cafe, 239 Shepherd of the Hills Expressway. 336-5668. Open for lunch and dinner Wednesday through Saturday, full bar, entertainment.

Devil's Pool Restaurant

Located in the fantastic Big Cedar Lodge, the Devil's Pool Restaurant is making waves as one of the finest dining establishments in town. Trout is a specialty here and will always continue to be as long as it is prepared as expertly as it is now, but the diner can also find delicious steaks, prime rib, pastas, pork tenderloin, and wonderful appetizers.

It is not uncommon to see local as well as out-of-town performers dining at the Devil's Pool. Breakfast, lunch, and dinner lures significant numbers to this fine restaurant.

During our visit to the Devil's Pool Restaurant, a waiter related a local tale about the name. Devil's Pool Spring, located a short distance from the facility, was supposedly where the bodies of a number of law enforcement officers were dumped during the 1930s. Old-timers who live in the area say the story is true.

Devil's Pool Restaurant is part of the Big Cedar Lodge Complex located at 612 Devil's Pool Road. 335-5141.

Dillon's Pub

Dillon's is a place well known to Branson locals and is considered one of the primo hangouts for folks who like pool, burgers, and friendly conversation, not necessarily in that order.

One can expect to find more locals at Dillon's than tourists. The advantage of this is that those who regularly dine at Dillon's can provide all kinds of information on the great burgers listed on the menu as well as what's going on around town. Speaking of burgers, Dillon's has more different kinds of hamburgers and cheeseburgers than anyplace else in Branson, and maybe Missouri!

Dillon's Pub. 309 East Main Street. 334-9651.

Dimitri's

Dimitri's is located on Lake Taneycomo. Not on the shore, but actually on the water itself. This great restaurant is housed on an old barge that floats out on the surface of the water but is securely attached to the bank.

Greek food is what you will find here, and it includes some of the finest manifestations of that cuisine found anywhere. This is the real thing, cooked and served up the way it is done in Greece and in Greek communities throughout the United States.

Lamb, of course, will be on the menu at Dimitri's, but the diner will also discover excellent steaks, seafood, and pasta. A great plus at Dimitri's is the attractive china, silverware, and glassware. These folks know how to treat the guest to an exquisite meal. This is a great place to take people you want to impress.

Dimitri's is located at 500 East Main. For reservations call 334-0888.

Dixie Stampede

Owner and country-western superstar Dolly Parton guarantees the Dixie Stampede is the "most fun place to eat for families!" Attractive menu selections and four-course feasts are available for all members of the family as they watch an action-packed show. Rotisserie chicken and smoked pork ribs are a favorite here, and understandably so. Kids especially love the Dixie Stampede.

The Dixie Stampede is located at 1527 76 Country Boulevard. For reservations call (417) 336-3000 or 1-800-520-5544.

Bob Evans Restaurant

This is a favorite place for breakfast, lunch, or dinner, seven days a week. The numbers of regulars who eat here can't be wrong. The Bob Evans Restaurant is spacious, friendly, sparkling clean, and features some of the best home-style cooking in this part of the Ozarks. Some claim the biscuits here are the best anywhere! And how long has it been since you've had fried mush? Well, you can get it at Bob Evans, and it's good, too. Senior menus with special deals are a favorite here, and there are also kids menus available. Prices are very reasonable.

The Bob Evans Restaurant is located at 801 West Main Street. For information call (417)336-2023.

Country Kitchen

This fine restaurant is located right across the street from the Osmond Family Theater. What more could you want: great food, reasonable prices, full buffet, regular and senior menu, and live entertainment. Open seven days a week from 6:30 A.M. until midnight.

The Country Kitchen is located at 3225 76 Country Boulevard. For information call (417) 334-2766.

Fall Creek Steakhouse

Hickory-grilled steaks are the main attraction here, and that seems to be enough to draw in hordes of hungry customers. Other fine menu items are available, but the steaks are the headliner at this fine place.

Fall Creek Steakhouse is located at Fall Creek Road and Missouri Highway 165. Open seven days a week, lunch and dinner. For information call (417) 336-5060.

Farmhouse Restaurant

The Farmhouse is the first place I ever ate in Branson, and I keep coming back to it every trip. My favorite meal here is the chicken-fried steak, but locals brag confidently about the catfish, chicken livers, and breakfast.

Whatever becomes your favorite at the Farmhouse, the dish that earned this popular downtown cafe its area-wide reputation is the blackberry cobbler—none better anywhere.

The Farmhouse Restaurant is located at 119 West Main Street. For information call 334-9701.

The Farmhouse Restaurant

Friendship House

Another regular stop during visits to Branson and surrounding environs is the Friendship House, a great restaurant on the edge of the College of the Ozarks campus. Breakfast, lunch, and dinner are served Monday through Saturday; breakfast and lunch only are served on Sunday.

This simple yet spacious and satisfying restaurant is staffed by students at the College of the Ozarks. One can order from the menu or stock up from the buffet. Either way, the meal will be one of the most satisfying you will encounter in this area.

During the past few years, the Friendship House has gained a well-deserved reputation for its burgers, breakfast, and the ice cream made at the nearby college-operated dairy.

A souvenir shop is also housed in the same building as the restaurant.

The Friendship House is located at the entrance to the College of the Ozarks in Hollister. For information call (417) 334-6411.

Garcia's Mexican Restaurant

If you like Mexican food, you will love Garcia's. This is the real thing, done up right and quite acceptable to the tastes of southwest Missourians and visitors from all over. It's all here: tamales, enchiladas, chimichangas, burritos, and a number of other excellent dishes you have never heard of but will want to try.

This fine restaurant has a lot to offer. In the first place, it is owned and operated by first-generation Mexicans who know a lot about cooking, how to serve it, and what people like to eat. In the second place, it is friendly, and the diner not only feels welcome, but also wants to stay for a while. In the third place, eating at Garcia's is fun and satisfying.

Garcia's Mexican Restaurant, open seven days a week, is located at 3016 76 Country Boulevard, serves lunch and dinner, and has a full bar and a kids menu. For information call (417) 334-5801.

Gilley's Texas Cafe and Cantina

Award-winning entertainer Mickey Gilley decided what Branson needed most of all was a Texas-style eatery. He has succeeded with Gilley's Texas Cafe, and you will agree when you try the Texas-style fajitas, ribs, steaks, chicken, chili, sandwiches, and more.

Gilley's Texas Cafe is located at 3457 76 Country Boulevard. For information call (417) 335-2755.

Guitars and Cadillacs

Open for lunch at 11:00 A.M., Guitars and Cadillacs features some of the finest sandwiches, soups, and salads in town. Sandwich lovers in and around Branson talk up the G & C's famous tenderloin sandwich, and it's everything they say it is. I heard about this restaurant's tenderloin sandwich in Kansas City!

In the evening, you can not only get a great meal, but also enjoy line dancing. This is a great place for beginners to learn and for folks to just watch the wide and entertaining variety of people who come through the doors.

Guitars and Cadillacs is located at the intersection of Highways 65 and 248. For information call (417) 335-7881.

Hard Luck Diner

Described as "good ol' fashioned food and fun," the Hard Luck Diner lives up to its excellent reputation, always delivering the goods as what many call Branson's most entertaining restaurant. Along with the exciting menu, waiters and waitresses spontaneously broke out into song during our visit. In addition to the great food served here, the Hard Luck Diner also features a wonderful soda fountain with all you favorite malts, shakes, sundaes, and other tasty desserts.

The Hard Luck is open seven days a week for breakfast, lunch, and dinner and is located in the Grand Village Shopping Center on Highway 76 next to the Grand Palace. For information call (417) 336-SHOP.

Home Cannery Restaurant

The Home Cannery is a nice, clean, and friendly place that features a full menu and a great buffet. The breakfast buffet here is especially popular with Bransonites and visitors alike and serves up a hearty mix of all your favorites including grits, gravy, sausage, eggs, and homemade cinnamon rolls. The lunch buffet generally features delicious fried chicken, ribs, a deli sandwich bar, and some of the best bread pudding this side of Louisiana. The dinner buffet features hand-carved roast beef and ham, catfish, homemade casseroles, and wonderful desserts.

The Home Cannery Restaurant is located in the Edgewood Motel at 1810 76 Country Boulevard. For information call 334-6965.

Hong Kong Buffet

The Hong Kong Buffet brings to the diner all the Chinese cuisine standards one expects in a fine restaurant. All of the items on the buffet are prepared without monosodium glutamate, and the price is just right—the Hong Kong may have one of the best lunch deals in town.

Particularly excellent here is the beef with oyster sauce. The chow meins and chop sueys are as good as any and better than most.

The Hong King Buffet is located at 1208 76 Country Boulevard. For information call (417) 334-2727.

Jake's Rib House

Open every day, Jake's serves up a fine basic barbecue that remains popular with a lot of Branson-area residents. Smoked on hickory wood, the beef, pork, and ribs go fast, so get there early. All of the side dishes one expects with barbecue are available. Prices are extremely reasonable.

Jake's Rib House is located out on Missouri Highway 376. For information call (417) 334-4947.

James and Blake

James and Blake is a relatively new place that offers a variety of coffees, cappuccinos, mochas, and lattes, as well a number of tasty and filling menu items.

We learned about James and Blake from several folks who work at various retail establishments in Branson. The word they provided was that, though James and Blake offers breakfast, lunch, and dinner, they have one of the best lunches in town at some of the most affordable prices. Vegetarian selections are also available, as are bagels.

James and Blake is located at 113 West Main Street. For more information call (417) 339-3032.

The *Lake Queen*

How about a great meal on Branson's original stern-wheeler? For something truly different, truly delightful, climb aboard this impressive paddle wheeler and sample the breakfast, lunch, or dinner buffet while you tour Lake Taneycomo and listen to some live entertainment. There are six cruises daily, and lakefront vistas, bluffs, peaceful coves, and wildlife pleasantly greet the diner.

To reach The *Lake Queen*, drive to 280 North Lake Drive. For more information call (417) 334-3015.

Lone Star Steakhouse

Atmosphere and flat-out fun are some of the attractions at the Lone Star Steakhouse, but the real stars are the steaks themselves.

While you're dining on any of the fine mesquite-grilled steaks, chicken, and hamburgers and filling up on the excellent black bean soup or Amarillo cheese fries, the waitresses may suddenly burst out into song, and two or three of them might team up spontaneously and start dancing for you.

A loose, friendly, yet efficient staff helps provide for fun and frolic at this charming restaurant.

The Lone Star Steakhouse is located at 201 Wildwood Drive. For more information call (417) 336-5030.

Lotus Valley

The operators of the Lotus Valley are in cahoots with the same folks who run the Hong Kong Buffet. The same excellent food and service can be found here with the addition of several extra entrees. Lunch and dinner at the Lotus Valley are popular with visitors.

The Lotus Valley is located at 3129 76 Country Boulevard. For more information call (417) 334-3427.

Lowes Fall Creek Steakhouse

For lunch or dinner, the steaks at Lowes are thick, cooked over hickory, and darned delicious. The menu features a number of other tempting entrees, but the steaks are the reason to eat here.

Lowes is also called Branson's home of the tossed rolls. It's true; if you need a roll with your dinner, the waiter tosses it to you! If you miss, don't worry about it—he'll just toss you another one!

Lowes Fall Creek Steakhouse is located at the intersection of Missouri Highway 165 and Fall Creek Road. For more information call (417) 336-5060.

Ashley Mayes

Located at the Grand Ramada, this place features fine food, excellent service, and rooftop dining.

Ashley Mayes is located at 245 Wildwood. For information call (417) 339-0050.

McFarlain's Bakery and Pie Shop

Open for breakfast, lunch, and dinner, this place advertises "Ozark Cookin' Like It's Spose Ta Be!" If you like home cooking, this is certainly the place to go. McFarlain's offers some esoteric items such as fried green tomatoes, french-fried sweet potatoes, and something called the Ozark noodle bake. These dishes are not only fun, they are goooood! Deserts at McFarlain's are in a class by themselves. In fact, this establishment is rather famous in this part of Missouri for its pies. One taste and you will understand why.

McFarlain's also features a "Back Porch" express deli. Here, one can find "wagon wheel" pizzas, "flap" sandwiches, and a great soda fountain.

McFarlain's Bakery and Pie Shop is located at 3562 Shepherd of the Hills Expressway. For more information call (417) 336-4680.

McGuffey's

The first time I ate at the McGuffey's located near the Andy Williams Theater, I actually saw Andy Williams himself dining there. Although McGuffey's offers some extremely tasty pasta dishes and fine sandwiches, the great burgers remain the favorite here, both with visitors and the regular diners. Open for lunch and dinner (only the Wildwood location serves breakfast), McGuffey's never disappoints, and folks find themselves returning again and again.

By the way, McGuffey's bar, the Faculty Lounge, is a great place for evening gatherings and spirited conversations.

Branson boasts four McGuffey's locations: 2600 76 Country Boulevard. (417) 336-3600, 3265 Falls Parkway. (417) 337-5389, 1464 West Missouri Highway 248. (417) 335-8680, and 120 Wildwood Drive. (417) 336-4156.

Mesquite Charlie's

Mesquite Charlie's boldly advertises "We've Got The Best Steaks In The Country," and a number of locals claim it's true. The aged steaks are cut daily and, if you like, grilled over aromatic mesquite wood. Featured here are a 32-ounce Porterhouse T-bone as well as smaller T-bones, a 16-ounce ribeye, and a 16-ounce New York strip.

Folks also come to Mesquite Charlie's for tasty fare other than steaks. The barbecued baby back ribs would bring a smile to the face of any aficionado, and the chicken and seafood are also well worth the trip.

The old-time western atmosphere is a lot of fun at Mesquite Charlie's. There is a western saloon that features a number of bronze Remingtons. The restaurant, described as family-style, seats over 1,200.

Mesquite Charlie's is located at the intersection of Gretna Road and Roark Valley Road. For more information call (417) 334-0498.

Midtown Diner

While this popular eatery, open daily from 11:00 A.M. to 2:00 P.M. and from 4:00 P.M. until the last diner leaves, features a number of wonderful menu items, folks flock to the Midtown time and again for the stellar buffet, the super sandwiches, and the big, juicy hamburgers. Many claim the Midtown has the best dinner buffet in town; the catfish, ribs, roast beef, and shrimp draw a lot of repeat customers. Others dare you to find a better homemade cobbler. Specials include meatloaf, chicken-fried steak, shrimp, and steak. Whatever you select to eat here, you will not go away from the Midtown disappointed.

The Midtown Diner is located at 1580 76 Country Boulevard.

Mr. G's Chicago-Style Pizza

This fine eatery serves up incredibly tasty pizza to a large number of faithful customers. If you like authentic pizza—not that franchise stuff—this is the place to go. Crust, sauce, and breads are all homemade, and the combinations of delicious ingredients you can get on your pizza is endless.

Mr. G's is located at 202 1/2 North Commercial. For more information call (417) 335-8156.

Old Apple Mill Restaurant

At the Old Apple Mill Restaurant, you get plates and platters heaped with delicious food, all home-style cooking, all delicious. Here they serve meatloaf the way your grandmother made it and fried chicken the way it is supposed to be cooked. Nobody, and I mean nobody, ever goes away from the Old Apple Mill hungry or unsatisfied.

The Old Apple Mill Restaurant is located at 3009 76 Country Boulevard. For more information call (417) 334-6090.

Ozark Family Restaurant

In business for over twenty-five years, the Ozark Family Restaurant features breakfast, lunch, and dinner buffets. Wide and varied selections are the ticket here, and the prices are as appealing as the food.

Particularly noteworthy is the all-you-can-eat seafood buffet. You know a seafood buffet is good when local citizens return over and over again for the fare.

The Ozark Family Restaurant is located at 1580 76 Country Boulevard. For more information call (417) 334-1206.

Ozark Mountain Buffet

The first time we entered the Ozark Mountain Buffet, the steam table looked like it was fifty yards long. Not quite, but what was even more impressive was what we found on it—ribs, roast beef, chicken, pasta, and even Cajun food. The chicken, we noticed, went fast. After sampling some of it, we understood why.

This is no ordinary buffet. The food here is of incredibly high quality, very tasty, and surprisingly inexpensive.

The Ozark Mountain Buffet is located at 3099 Shepherd of the Hills Expressway. For more information call (417) 335-5811.

Paradise Grill and Bar

Fine California-style food, friendly service, fun family dining, a generous buffet and full menu highlight this enjoyable restaurant. On the menu, one will find many eclectic selections, and the greatest difficulty will be choosing between them. The word around Branson is to go to the Paradise for appetizers—the best in town, we are told. All of the meals are skillfully prepared, salads are fresh, and the salad dressings are homemade.

The Paradise Grill has been moved to the top of our list as a place to stop every time we visit Branson. It is located at 3250 Shepherd of the Hills Expressway in the motel next door to the Shoji Tabuchi Theater. For more information call (417) 334-5405.

The Pasta House

Located just behind the Grand Palace, The Pasta House Italian restaurant is open for lunch and dinner seven days a week. In recent months, the Pasta House bar has been a favorite gathering place for lots of folks who are looking for a bite to eat and a drink or two after watching some of the shows.

The Pasta House is located at 2690 Green Mountain Drive. For more information call (417) 337-9882.

Penelope's Family Restaurant

Penelope's is yet another fine example of a local restaurant that serves up delicious family-style cooking. A popular eatery for a lot of Branson visitors, the two locations are convenient to shows and shopping.

Many Branson restaurants have their fans, and Penelope's is no exception. Locals tout the breakfasts, and when word gets out about the lunches and dinners, the parking lots at these two fine places begin to fill up.

There are two Penelope's Family Restaurants. One is located at 3015 76 Country Boulevard. (417) 334-3335. The other can be found at 103 Commercial Street. (417) 334-4444.

Pepper Bellies

One of the most popular styles of Mexican food sweeping the country these days is Jalisco style, and you can find a prime example of this stunning cuisine right here in Branson. Fresh and delicious salsa greets the diner, and it all gets better from there.

A positive recommendation for a restaurant is when the locals eat there. Lots and lots of local businessmen, clerks, real estate salespeople, and even sheetrock hangers and truck drivers dine regularly at Pepper Bellies and continue to come back again and again.

Pepper Bellies is located at 305 Main Street close to Lake Tanycomo. Open seven days a week for lunch and dinner. No credit cards. For more information call (417) 339-4096.

Peppercorn's Restaurant and Bakery

Good-looking and good-tasting breakfasts, lunches, and dinners greet the visitor to Peppercorn's, housed in an attractive Victorian-style building right across from the Andy Williams Theater. Peppercorn's is famous for its chicken, but one of the main attractions here is the baked trout almondine glazed with butter and served on a bed of rice—simply scrumptious. The prime rib is also a specialty and has drawn raves from hundreds.

Peppercorn's is located at 2421 West Highway 76 Country Boulevard. For information call (417) 335-6699.

The Plantation Restaurant

The Plantation was voted the Number One restaurant in Branson for three years in a row. Delicious is a word that can be applied to virtually everything on the menu and buffet here. If you don't believe me, ask BoxCar Willie, who is a regular diner at this fine restaurant. In fact, he has been at the Plantation every time we've hit for lunch. The restaurant, by the way, is only a short walk from the BoxCar Willie Theater. Be sure to try the freshwater catfish, the fine steaks and ribs, and the pan-fried chicken. Alcohol is also available.

The Plantation is located next door to the BoxCar Willie Theater at 3460 76 Country Boulevard. For information call (417) 334-7800.

Pzazz

At Pzazz, the diner finds a sports theme throughout, even applied to most of the menu items ("World Series" pizza, for example). Jack Hamilton, the owner, is a former professional baseball player, and he has struck gold with this fine restaurant. The Pzazz pizzas are some of the best to be found anywhere, and all are made completely from scratch. The aforementioned World Series pizza may be the only pizza ever made with prime rib! Absolutely delicious.

Sports-oriented diners, as well as linksters from the nearby golf course, have the time of their lives at Pzazz, and the bar is a great evening hangout.

Pzazz is located at 158 Pointe Royale Drive. For more information call (417) 335-2798.

The Rails

Some of the most outstanding seafood and Cajun food in the region can be found right here at The Rails. We spoke with a tour bus driver in another city who said his riders, many of them repeat customers, insist on stopping at The Rails for a meal.

The fare includes a number of Cajun dishes such as gumbo but also features clam strips, catfish, grilled chicken, shrimp (fried or peel-'em-and-eat-'em), and cobbler. Dinner only, buffet and menu.

The Rails is located at 433 Animal Safari Road just off Missouri Highway 165. For more information call (417) 336-3401.

Rocky's Italian Restaurant

I was first introduced to Rocky's Italian Restaurant by some local residents, who said it was "the best-kept dining secret in Branson." If they keep serving the fine fare I sampled during my visit, they won't be a secret for long.

The toasted ravioli is made fresh and was a big hit with everyone in the restaurant during a recent visit. Bread is also made fresh daily.

With a complete Italian menu and an impressive wine list, Rocky's has just about everything the serious diner of Italian cuisine needs.

Rocky's Italian Restaurant is located at 120 North Sycamore Road. For information call (417) 335-4765.

Rose Garden Restaurant

The food at the Rose Garden is well worth the six-mile drive to the little town of Walnut Shade. The scenery and ambience is a giant bonus. Waterfalls, chandeliers, and high ceilings are impressive. Regulars at the Rose Garden will tell you that you can't find a better buffet—whether breakfast, lunch, or dinner—anywhere in Missouri.

Wine drinkers are particularly fond of the Rose Garden—a wide selection of wine is available. The Sunday champagne brunch is one of the finest we have ever indulged in.

While the food at the Rose Garden is of the highest quality, the prices are extremely reasonable.

The Rose Garden Restaurant is located at 485 Rose O'Neill Road in Walnut Shade. For more information call (417) 561-2250.

Ruby Tuesday

This incredibly popular chain offers its noted burgers, ribs, and grilled chicken but also features some local favorites such as trout. Many fans of Ruby Tuesday come back time and again for the salad bar and the desserts. The salad bar, incidentally, may be the best in a town that claims many great ones. Ruby Tuesday is a favorite with families, couples, and kids—a little bit of everything can be found here, and everything is guaranteed to please.

Ruby Tuesday is located at 3316 76 Country Boulevard. For more information call (417) 335-5450.

Sadie's Sideboard

Since 1982, Sadie's, according to hundreds of visitors, has provided some of the best food and service to be found anywhere in the Ozarks. Families return to this great restaurant year in and year out. Some of the waitresses can even call annual visitors by name!

Most folks who dine at Sadie's come for the stupendous all-you-can-eat buffets—breakfast, lunch, and dinner. The breakfast buffet features Sadie's own delicious griddlecakes with syrup, along with a choice of excellent meats, eggs, muffins, biscuits, and gravy. The dinner buffet generally includes tasty fried chicken, roast beef, ribs, homemade rolls, and a variety of vegetables and desserts. While dining at Sadie's, be sure to try some of her famous homemade chicken noodle soup.

Sadie's Sideboard is located across the street from the Baldknobbers Theater at 2840 76 Country Boulevard. For information call (417) 334-3619.

Scherlings Cowboy Cafe

Offering a great buffet, a complete menu, and a full-service bar, this cafe is located across the street from the Magic Mansion. Every Wednesday is blues jam night.

Scherlings Cowboy Cafe is located at 526 Shepherd of the Hills Expressway.

The Shack Cafe

This is one of the better old-timey downtown cafes you will find in Branson. You're going to get basic food here, nothing fancy, but man, is it ever good. Breakfast, lunch, and dinner are all a treat. The last time I breakfasted at the Shack, the cinnamon roll was so big I couldn't eat all of it. Whatever you have for lunch or dinner (burgers are recommended), be sure you get a piece of pie to accompany it—you won't be sorry.

Open Monday through Saturday, The Shack Cafe has some of the friendliest waitresses in town, and that's saying something.

The Shack Cafe is located at 108 South Commercial Street. For information call (417) 334-3490.

Showboat Branson Belle

A two-hour cruise on Table Rock Lake in an impressive 1890s vintage paddle wheeler is a treat anytime. Add to this event a fine meal, and you have a combination that is hard to beat. Breakfast, lunch, and dinner excursions are available, and all of the food is prepared fresh in the boat's galley. Call for reservations.

To reach the *Showboat Branson Belle*, drive down Missouri Highway 165 near Table Rock Dam and look for the signs. For information call (417) 336-7171.

Simon's Cafe

This friendly, family-oriented restaurant is open seven days a week for breakfast, and Monday through Saturday for dinner. American and Mexican food are specialties here, and Friday and Saturday evenings feature a darned good Mexican buffet.

Simon's Cafe is located at 2939 76 Country Boulevard. For more information call (417) 335-4905.

Spaghettatas

Spaghetti, fettuccini, lasagna, and other kinds of pasta are all here, all delicious, and all appropriately priced. Portions are extremely generous, and if you leave this place hungry, you have nobody to blame but yourself.

While the pasta is what made this place noted, the prime rib and steak dishes are also excellent. A big hit here is the fresh bread that is served hot just as it comes out of the oven.

Located just behind The Grand Palace, Spaghettatas is open for dinner only, contains an excellent bar, and sports a list of good wines.

Spaghettatas is located at 2805 Green Mountain drive. For more information call (417) 336-4905.

Stage Door Canteen

This fine eatery is the setting for the popular Lennon Brothers Breakfast Show. Great live entertainment along with quality food await the morning diner here.

Lunch and dinner are also very popular with folks staying at the Welk Resort, as well as drop-ins. Roast turkey with walnut dressing and gravy is a favorite, and the seafood is attracting more and more folks as word gets out.

The Stage Door Canteen is located in the Welk Resort Center at 1984 Missouri Highway 165. For more information call (417) 336-3575.

Starvin' Marvin's Family Restaurant

Pretty darned good home cooked meals can be found at Starvin' Marvin's, with the fried chicken a big hit with everyone. Many restaurants in Branson claim to have the best fried chicken in town, but, as one local relates, "If they took a vote, Starvin' Marvin's would win hands down!"

Starvin' Marvin's Family Restaurant is located at 3340 76 Country Boulevard. For information call (417) 334-7402.

Tran's Oriental Restaurant

Tran's offers some fine selections for lunch and dinner, selections that are extolled by many of the locals who eat here. For around five bucks, a fine lunch can be purchased. Dinner selections are wide and varied, food is plentiful, and the prices are quite low.

Tran's Oriental Restaurant is located at 1305 76 Country Boulevard. For information call (417) 334-4652.

Uncle Joe's Bar-B-Q Restaurant

Some are drawn to Uncle Joe's for barbecue as a result of the great reputation of this restaurant. Some pull into the parking lot when they smell the tantalizing hickory smoke wafting across the landscape. When President George Bush, who is rumored to know his barbecue, visited this area in 1992, he was also lured by the aroma and stopped to order a couple of rib lunches. Whatever the reason for arriving at Uncle Joe's, you are sure to find some of the finest examples of Ozark barbecued ribs, brisket, pork, and ham. In addition, Uncle Joe's features some great-tasting pasta and prime rib. Wine and beer are available, as are bottles of Uncle Joe's famous barbecue sauce.

Uncle Joe's Bar-B-Q Restaurant is located at 2818 76 Country Boulevard. For information call (417) 334-4548.

Upstairs at Jim Stafford's

Rumor has it that entertainer Jim Stafford was so enamored of the food served in the restaurant in an adjacent town that he coaxed the cook to come to Branson to prepare meals at his theater for him and his visitors. The food here can best be described as light and delicious—crab salad, chilled strawberry soup, a variety of muffins, as well as a number of attractive entrees. The restaurant is open seven days a week for dinner and for lunch during matinees.

Upstairs at Jim Staffords is located at 3440 76 Country Boulevard. For information call (417) 335-8080.

Uptown Cafe

The first thing one notices on entering the Uptown Cafe is the wallpaper and marble floors and the somewhat art deco look about the place. I liked it because for some reason I've always had good food at an art deco type of restaurant.

That strange tradition held up here at the Uptown. Steakburgers, hamburgers, brisket sandwiches, meatloaf, and chicken-fried steak draw customers back again and again for all the right reasons.

The Uptown Cafe is located at 285 South Missouri 165. For information call (417) 336-3535.

Windy City Dogs

Chicago-style hot dogs are the lure at Windy City. Since locals and visitors alike are well aware of the fine selection of hot dogs here, lunch can be a little busy, so come early. If hot dogs are not your style, a number of sandwiches are also available, including pita sandwiches.

Kids and adults alike love Windy City.

Windy City Dogs is located at 315 East Main Street. For information call (417) 335-3748.

Wooden Nickel Restaurant

The *New York Times* called the Wooden Nickel Restaurant one of the best places to dine in Branson. An extremely successful operation in business for over two decades, the Wooden Nickel does, in fact, provide some of the finest dining anywhere in the Ozarks. Seafood, prime rib, baby back ribs, and frog legs are just a few of the excellent dishes prepared and served here.

The salad bar at the Wooden Nickel is worth the trip to this restaurant. Constructed around an oak tree and decorated with handcrafted copper leaves and flowers, this unique feature dominates the spacious dining room.

A word about the steaks: The Wooden Nickel does not serve ordinary steaks. No sir. All of the steaks served here are aged and come from corn-fed Iowa cattle. None better anywhere in this part of Missouri.

The Wooden Nickel Restaurant is located one mile west of Silver Dollar City on Missouri Highway 76. For information call (417) 338-2737.

Worman House Restaurant

The Worman House Restaurant located at Big Cedar Lodge is a place you will want to consider visiting if you are in the mood for what one recent visitor called "the meal of a lifetime." Supervised and prepared by a real chef, dinners at the Worman House tend to be a bit pricey compared to the average tourist dining-out budget, but well worth every cent invested.

The pan-seared grouper is comparable to that found in the finest of eateries in Key West. The rack of lamb is served with an incredibly delicious sauce—more an exciting experience than a simple meal.

The Sunday brunch at the Worman House is also gaining raves from visitors. Whether you select dinner or brunch or both, be sure you make reservations.

The Worman House Restaurant is located in the Big Cedar Lodge at 612 Devil's Pool Road. For information call (417) 339-5200.

In addition to all of the fine restaurants and cafes listed above, Branson also has a number of well-known and highly respected franchise outlets. A lot of visitors to this exciting city take comfort in eating out at places that are familiar to them, places similar to the ones they dine at in their hometowns.

Branson's popular franchise restaurants include: Bonanza, Cracker Barrel, Golden Corral, Kentucky Fried Chicken, Landry's Seafood House (fish, shrimp, Cajun), Olive Garden Restaurant (Italian), Outback (steaks, alligator tail, alcohol) The Pasta House Company (Italian), Shorty Small's (steaks, burgers, brisket, cheese sticks, cocktails, children's menu), and Steak and Shake.

Places To Stay: Hotels, Motels, Condos, Resorts, Inns, and Bed and Breakfasts

During the early settlement period of Branson when the primary attraction for visitors was the fishing, there were a few nice fishing camps and resorts, along with a small number of motels and courts, where travelers stayed.

As the years passed and the music and entertainment industry began to grow rapidly during the sixties and seventies, it was accompanied by a corresponding demand for more, better, and more diverse accommodations. Recognizing this important need, major hotel and motel chains moved to Branson to establish suitable lodging for the increasing numbers of visitors. As it became clear that Branson would soon rival Nashville and Las Vegas as a major United States tourist attraction, other investors began to examine the area, and most of them soon proceeded with designs and construction of hotels, motels, and inns.

Today, some of the finest accommodations in the country can be found in Branson, ranging from small, quiet downtown hotels to countryside bed and breakfasts to large complexes featuring everything from basic rooms to

227

multiple-room suites with fireplaces and Jacuzzis. Some hotels even feature diversions such as horseback riding and volleyball.

It can truly be said that there is something for everybody in Branson, and that certainly includes places to stay. Everything from budget-level accommodations to the most luxurious rooms and accessories in the country can be found here.

Allendale Resort

The Allendale Resort has been around for about eight decades and over the years has served many of Lake Taneycomo's most avid fishermen. Today, the sons and grandsons of fishermen who came here during the thirties and forties register at the Allendale. If you stay here, you have the best of both worlds—the lake for fishing and boating, and downtown Branson.

The cabins are rustic and charming, but all have central heat and air as well as cable television. The Allendale Resort is a very comfortable and efficient place to stay, and in spite of its great tradition and longevity, the rates at the Allendale are among the most reasonable in town.

For information write to Allendale Resort, 411 North Commercial Street, Branson 65616, or call (417) 334-3327.

Alpenrose Motor Inn

A kind of a Bavarian-type place, the fifty-room Alpenrose is many things—fun, pleasant, comfortable, reasonably priced, and a pure delight. When you register for your room in the cheery, spacious lobby, you will no doubt notice the fine original art hanging on the walls. All of the art works are the products of local artists. Everything is for sale, and some great bargains can be found here.

The Alpenrose is one of several Branson area motels that get a lot of positive word-of-mouth recommendations around the country from previous visitors. There is an outdoor swimming pool here, and you can challenge your kids to a game of miniature golf at the Pirate's Cove next door.

For more information write to the Alpenrose Motor Inn, 2875 Green Mountain Drive, Branson, Missouri 65616, or call 1-800-324-9494.

Amber Light Motor Inn

Fast becoming a favorite place to stay in Branson among many regular visitors, the Amber Light has a rather unique setting. After you check in, you drive around behind the office and then down the hill along a woodsy kind of road to the units. The peace and quiet is appealing and quite comfortable down here. And you can be content in knowing you are mere minutes away from shows and restaurants.

The Amber Light has a nice outdoor swimming pool, and each of the units has cable television. Free coffee awaits you in the office in the morning.

For more information write to the Amber Light Motor Inn, 1945 76 Country Boulevard, Branson, Missouri, or call (417) 334-7200.

Artilla Cove Resort

The comfortable accommodations at the Artilla Cove Resort are nicely appointed, and each one of them has a gorgeous view of Table Rock Lake. Only a mile and a half from Silver Dollar City and a few minutes more to downtown Branson, the Artilla Cove Resort is perceived as an ideal location by many travelers.

Fishermen likewise enjoy the Artilla Cove Resort. A covered and lighted boat dock and concrete boat ramp are located only a few steps from the resort, and the fertile waters of Table Rock Lake beckon bass fishermen. Boat and motor rental are also available.

A great getaway place, the Artilla features a swimming pool, guest laundry, and a playground for the children. For more information write HC 1, Box 839, Branson, Missouri 65616-9604 or call (417) 338-2346.

Atrium Inn

As you might expect, a large and attractive atrium dominates the lobby of this place. The Atrium has an outdoor pool, cable TV, and a lot of the other things you expect to find in a quality inn these days. Among the best features of the Atrium Inn, according to many who have stayed here, are the deli and ice cream parlor!

For information or reservations, write to the Atrium Inn, 3005 Green Mountain Drive, Broans, Missouri 65616 or call 1-800-656-5555.

Aunt Sadie's Garden Glade B & B

Nicely and quietly located in the woods on a gravel road well off U.S. Highway 65, Aunt Sadie's is the place you want to go if you would like to be treated like a king. Or a queen.

Folks who have stayed here have raved about the country breakfasts they were served. The rooms are great, too—some have hot tubs, some have fireplaces.

Aunt Sadie's is a clean, comfortable place that is ideal for peace and quiet. On the other hand, when you are ready for a show or a big dinner in town, you are only a few short miles away from the action.

For reservations write to Aunt Sadie's Garden Glade B & B, 163 Fountain Street, or call 1-800-944-4250.

Aunt Mollie's Boarding House

Aunt Mollie was one of the main characters in Harold Bell Wright's play *The Shepherd of the Hills*. These clean, low-priced units named after her are very comfortable and only a few minutes from downtown Branson. Included in your rate are two breakfasts at the next-door restaurant. Aunt Mollie's offers an outdoor swimming pool and cable television.

For more information write to Aunt Mollie's Boarding House, 251 Expressway Lane or call (417) 334-0366.

Baldknobbers Motor Inn

Clearly intended to accommodate many of the thousands of visitors who come to Branson each year to visit the Baldknobbers Theater, the motor inn, as well as the restaurant, fills the bill nicely.

After you've seen the Baldknobbers show, the main road, which runs right in front of the inn, will take you virtually anyplace else you wish to go in Branson.

For information or reservations write to 2843 76 Country Boulevard, or call (417) 334-7948.

Barrington Hotel

Located not far from the Mel Tillis Theater, yet somewhat out of the stream of downtown traffic, the Barrington is a nice-looking, comfortable hotel with great rooms and a stunning lobby. There is a swimming pool, a continental breakfast, and cable television. Rooms with Jacuzzis are available.

For reservations and information write 263 Shepherd of the Hills Expressway or call 1-800-760-8866.

Ben's Wishing Well Motor Inn

Ben's is another of several conveniently located motels in this entertainment capital. Prices are very competitive at Ben's, and you are just across the street from Presleys' Jubilee Theater. Added attractions are a swimming pool and Jacuzzi.

For more information or to make reservations, write 2935 76 Country Boulevard or call 1-800-492-4344.

Best Western Music Capital Inn

This Best Western offers all the great service you have come to expect from this fine franchise. In addition to the ideal central location, the Best Western features an indoor pool, a sauna, fitness room, a gift shop (where you can purchase show tickets), and offers a continental breakfast.

For more information write to Best Western, 3257 Shepherd of the Hills Expressway, or call (417) 8378.

Big Cedar Lodge

If word-of-mouth means anything, Big Cedar Lodge may be the most gloriously luxurious place to stay when coming to Branson. A United States president selected Big Cedar Lodge when he visited here. Show business personalities from all over the world know that when coming to Branson, the Big Cedar is *the* place to stay for a few days. In fact, a trip to the Big Cedar Lodge can almost be a vacation in itself.

This is no ordinary hotel. In addition to the main lodge, the attractive and spacious log cabins, and the wonderful view overlooking Table Rock Lake, Big Cedar has within its 305 acres a riding stable, a great swimming pool, a marina, tennis courts, and impressive flower gardens.

Big Cedar is a bit pricey, but worth every penny spent here. As a development by the same folks who brought you the world-famous Bass Pro Shops, one can expect the same kind of quality. And quality is what you find at the Big Cedar—it is everywhere.

Big Cedar Lodge is also a great place for honeymooners, corporate executives, and just about anyone who craves an 'nth degree of class.

For reservations or information write to Big Cedar Lodge, 612 Devil's Pool Road, Ridgedale, Missouri, or call (417) 335-2777.

BoxCar Willie Motel Number One

Conveniently located directly behind the BoxCar Willie Theater, this comfortable motel employs a train theme. The visitor can follow the train tracks to the lobby or to the continental breakfast. In addition to the BoxCar Willie Theater, visitors are within walking distance to many great restaurants and other showplaces.

The prices are very reasonable and the service is friendly and efficient. For more information or reservations write 3454 76 Country Boulevard, or call (417) 334-8873.

BoxCar Willie Motel Number Two

Not far away from BoxCar Willie Motel Number One is BoxCar Willie Motel Number Two! A newer motel, this one also has a train theme, a swimming pool, the same fine service, reasonable prices, and a continental breakfast. Number Two also offers suites, king-size beds, and Jacuzzis.

For more information write 350 Schaefer Drive, Branson, Missouri 65616, or call 1-800-942-4626.

Bradford Inn

A few minutes out of Branson brings you to the Bradford Inn, a great place to stay with an incredible view. The rooms (and there are lots of options) are nicely appointed—some even have fireplaces, some have Jacuzzis, all have private decks or patios. There are lots of nice touches here, ranging from the murals on the walls to the journals in each room to the great breakfast.

The Bradford Inn is a family owned and operated enterprise. These folks are friendly, competent, and do everything imaginable to make the visitor feel comfortable.

For reservations or more information write Bradford Inn, Missouri Highway 265, Branson, or call 1-800-357-1466

Branson Hotel Bed and Breakfast

This old and historic building, nicely restored and remodeled, is conveniently located in downtown Branson. The nine rooms are exquisitely decorated and sparkling clean with lots of nice, personal touches and custom-made furniture, all made by local craftsmen.

Visitors to this classy building will enjoy sipping wine on the porch and watching the world go by just beyond. The breakfasts here are also gaining quite a positive reputation around town.

The Branson Hotel Bed and Breakfast is open March through November. For information and reservations write to 214 West Main Street, Branson, Missouri 65616, or call (417) 335-6104.

Branson House Bed and Breakfast Inn

The mother of the owner of the Branson Hotel Bed and Breakfast (see previous entry) owns this fine establishment. Here one has a choice of seven well-appointed rooms, a wide yard filled with nice big trees, and a comfortable porch.

One cannot help but be impressed with this operation—everything from ambience to rooms to breakfast. For information and reservations write to the Branson House Bed and Breakfast Inn, 120 Fourth Street, Branson, Missouri 65616, or call (417) 334-0959.

Cameron's Crag

Located in a quiet setting on Lake Taneycomo, Cameron's Crag has three rooms, all of which have king-size beds and hot tubs. Breakfasts are great here, and visitors are only a few minutes from downtown Branson.

For reservations or information write to Cameron's Crag at 738 Acadia Club Road, Point Lookout, Missouri, or call 1-800-933-8529.

Cascades Inn

The name "Cascades" comes from the waterfalls that greet the visitor to this nifty place.

There are two good reasons to stay at the Cascades Inn: First, the fine accommodations and convenient location offered by the friendly folks at the Cascades are well worth the stop. Second, the Paradise Grill, one of the better places to dine in Branson, is part of this 160-room hotel. Rooms with whirlpools or Jacuzzis may be reserved.

For reservations or more information write to the Cascades Inn at 3226 Shepherd of the Hills Expressway, or call 1-900-588-8424.

Cedar Resort

Located right on Table Rock Lake, Cedar Resort is close to Branson but far enough away to enjoy the quiet and calm of the woods and shore.

The Cedar Resort offers modern housekeeping cabins (all of which are air conditioned), cable television, swimming pool, lighted boat dock, boat and motor rental, playground, game room, and a laundry.

For information or reservations write to Cedar Resort, HCR 9, Box 1418, Branson, Missouri 65616.

Chateau On The Lake

This elegant, ten story, European-style resort looks like a castle when approached from Highway 265. Located a short distance north of Table Rock dam, this magnificent structure is ideally located in the middle of 135 wooded acres and cost over $45 million to construct.

The atrium in the Chateau is striking, featuring, among other things, a waterfall and handsome glass elevators. If you crave splendor during your stay in Branson, this is the place to be. This hotel also has a 35-seat movie theatre/teleconferencing room, spa, exercise room, an indoor as well as an outdoor pool, tennis courts, a supervised children's playground, a clothing store, a wonderful restaurant, and a deli. In addition, there are boat rentals, scuba diving, parasailing, and guided fishing expeditions out onto the nearby lake. If you don't like to drive, the Chateau offers shuttle service into town.

This is truly a four-star enterprise, and the prices of $160 to $270 ($460 for the presidential suite) are not at all out of line for all that is made available to the guests here.

Clarion Fall Creek Resort

This grand 350-condo-and-motel complex provides everything travelers might want in a home away from home, and all at reasonable prices to boot. There are indoor and outdoor swimming pools, a miniature golf course, exercise area, and continental breakfast. A marina on nearby Lake Taneycomo is handy for fishermen.

The location is quiet and out of the way of traffic but only minutes from downtown Branson. Write or call early for reservations at 1 Fall Creek Drive, or call (417) 334-6404.

Classic Motor Inn

As might be expected from the name, a 1950s classic car motif dominates this exciting motel—a fifties vintage Cadillac is parked in the lobby!

The rooms are very nice, and the Classic Motor Inn also features a swimming pool, coin-operated laundry, a gift shop, and a continental breakfast. Located near lots of shows, shopping, and dining, the Classic is a friendly place with great service.

For more information write to the Classic Motor Inn, 2384 Shepherd of the Hills Expressway, or call 1-800-334-6991.

Cooper Creek Resort and Campground

Located right on Lake Taneycomo, Cooper Creek Resort and Campground includes fourteen wooded acres of cabins and campsites. Only five minutes from the Branson entertainment strip, this cool, pleasant resort is always popular with fishermen and families.

One-, two-, and three-bedroom cabins are available, and all the cabins have decks and fully equipped kitchenettes. In addition, all linens are provided. The two swimming pools are popular with visitors, and there is also cable television, a coin-operated laundry, a grocery store, lighted fishing docks, a boat ramp, and boat and motor rentals.

Write for reservations at 471 Cooper Creek Road, Branson 65616, or call 1-800-261-8398.

Copper Tree Suites

Copper Tree Suites offers a little something different from the usual accommodations found in the region. The one and two roomy bedroom suites (as well as honeymoon suites), have in-room Jacuzzis, sofa sleepers, recliners, kitchenettes, and even fireplaces!

Conveniently located to all of the Branson activities, Copper Tree Suites are attractively set in the wooded Ozarks and are extremely clean.

For more information write Copper Tree Suites, 3706 West Highway 76, Branson, Missouri 65616, or call 1-800-358-9969.

The Cottage Resort

The Cottage is located a short distance off Highway 76 on an attractive peninsula that extends far out into Table Rock Lake. Individual roomy and well-appointed cottages are available. Year-round fishing for black bass, white bass, crappie, and perch is popular on this section of the lake, and a variety of water sports are easily and satisfactorily pursued here.

The Cottage Resort is very reasonably priced, and a number of different vacation packages are available. For more information write HCR 1, Box 1030B, Branson, Missouri 65616, or call 1-800-338-7228.

Crow's Nest Resort and Lodge

Located on Table Rock Lake, the Crow's Nest is quiet, clean, and convenient to downtown Branson. The lighted boat dock is handy for folks who want to go fishing, water skiing, or pleasure boating. The large swimming pool and surrounding area is perfect for relaxing after a day of shows and shopping.

For information or reservations write to the Crow's Nest Resort and Lodge, HCR 1, 792 SA, Branson, Missouri 65616, or call (417) 338-2524.

Deer Run Motel and Campground

If Silver Dollar City is your destination, then the Deer Run may be just the place for you. In fact, you can walk to SDC from your room in about two minutes!

Some rooms have kitchenettes, and nice suites are available. An outdoor swimming pool tempts one and all after a long day at Silver Dollar City.

A great bonus associated with the Deer Run is the shuttle service between the motel and Downtown Branson.

For more information or reservations call (417) 328-2223.

Dogwood Inn

The Dogwood Inn has long been a favored place to stay by Branson visitors. Located on 76 Country Boulevard, this place is within walking distance to a number of shows, yet it is remarkably quiet.

The Dogwood has 220 rooms (suites available), in-room coffee, laundry facilities and dry cleaning service, an outdoor pool, hot tub, fax and copy service, and gift shop. Kids stay free, and the restaurant is open for breakfast, lunch, and dinner.

There is a 2,500-square-foot fully supplied meeting room for conferences, which can be catered if you wish. The Dogwood has been the site of several reunions, and they are particularly helpful to tour groups.

The Dogwood Inn is located at 1420 76 Country Boulevard, Branson. Call (417) 334-5101 or (417) 334-0789 for information and reservations.

Edgewood Motel and Reunion Center

This 296-room motel, though conveniently located to shopping, music, and dining, is located adjacent to a nice, quiet park containing barbecue grills, picnic tables, and lots of room for the kids and the dog to run around. When you get enough of that, you can relax in the outdoor heated swimming pool or nap in a clean and spacious room.

My first introduction to the Edgewood Motel was as a guest of several musicians who were staying here. My first impressions were very positive, and I have returned several times to just enjoy the same fine accommodations. One of the best breakfasts in town, by the way, is located just a few steps from your room at the nearby Home Cannery Restaurant.

For more information write 1700 76 Country Boulevard, or call (417)334-1000.

Fall Creek Resort

The luxurious country club-like atmosphere encountered at this lovely lakeside resort claims many repeat visitors, and with good reason. This lovely location appeals to fishermen, honeymooners, and business executives alike. Indoor and outdoor pools are available, as are tennis courts, shuffleboard, a fitness center, and miniature golf. A full-service marina with boat and motor rental make fishing for prize-winning bass all the easier.

For more information or reservations call 1-800-56CONDO.

Good Shepherd Inn

A sixty-eight-room inn located close to the Branson action, the Good Shepherd Inn has reasonably priced, clean accommodations as well as free coffee down in the office in the morning. The owners will provide vacation package plans if you write to 1023 76 Country Boulevard, Branson, Missouri 65616, or call 1-800-324-3457.

Grand Oaks Hotel

The Grand Oaks, offering true luxury along with convenience, is located in the lovely Thousand Hills area. The Grand Oaks features an indoor pool, Jacuzzis, exercise room, game room, coin-operated laundry, security car-door locks, and a deluxe continental breakfast.

For information or reservations call 1-800-553-6423.

The Grand Victorian

Appropriately named, this neat place smacks of Victorian styles and colors. The outdoor pool stays busy during the warm summer months, and the indoor pool is a favorite relaxing place for folks who arrive during the cooler months. Rooms with Jacuzzis are available. There is also a video game room to keep the kids busy while you work out in the exercise room.

An excellent continental breakfast will be waiting for you each morning.

For information or reservations write to The Grand Victorian, 2325 76 Country Boulevard, Branson, Missouri 65616, or call (417) 336-2935.

Green Valley Resort

Close to Branson and Silver Dollar City, the Green Valley Resort is located just down the road in Reeds Spring and right on the shore of Table Rock Lake.

Here, the visitor can find fully equipped modern cabins with fireplaces, a swimming pool, hot tub, playground, a lighted boat dock, and a boat ramp.

The Green Valley Resort enjoys a fine reputation among visitors to the Branson area. For information or reservations write to the Green Valley Resort, HCR 4, Box 3470, Reeds Springs, Missouri 65737, or call 1-800-922-8156.

Hillbilly Inn Motel

Double beds and cable television are standard features in most of the Hillbilly Inn's fifty-one rooms. Located right on 76 Country Boulevard, this unique Inn has all of the rooms facing the woods in the opposite direction. Surprisingly quiet and very comfortable and convenient, the Hillbilly Inn Motel gets a lot of word-of-mouth advertising around the country from satisfied customers. Originally a general store, this nice motel has a certain rustic charm that appeals to most.

Rumor around Branson has it that entertainer Tony Orlando's favorite place for breakfast is the Hillbilly Inn breakfast bar.

For more information write 1166 76 Country Boulevard or call (417) 334-3946.

Holiday Hills Resort and Golf Club

The Holiday Hills Resort and Golf Club offers one-, two-, and three-bedroom condos with fully equipped kitchens, living rooms, dining rooms, Jacuzzi, and patio or balcony. Golfers particularly love the Holiday Hills and the eighteen-hole championship course, but more and more vacationers are discovering this fine facility is just a great place to get away for a few days.

In addition to the golf course, the Holiday Hills features two outdoor pools, a hot tub, horseshoe pitching, shuffleboard, tennis, archery range, basketball court, miniature golf, a pro shop, and fishing guide service.

For more information write to Holiday Hills Resort and Golf Club, 620 East Rockland Drive, Branson, Missouri 65616, or call 1-800-225-2422.

Holiday Inn Crowne Plaza

It is hard to believe this is a Holiday Inn. The Crowne Plaza version bears little resemblance to the famous national motel chain, but offers the same fine service and friendly, helpful staff. Even more so here, it seems.

Five hundred rooms can be found in this complex, each of them nicely appointed and featuring a coffeepot.

From the Crowne Plaza, you can see the Andy Williams Theater and the Grand Palace. Within short walking distance is a great shopping mall, the Grand Village. Swimming pools (indoor and outdoor) attract many, as do the spa, exercise room, and game room. There is even a hair salon.

The Holiday Inn Crowne Plaza is becoming the inn of choice for a number of businessmen who visit Branson on a regular basis.

For more information or reservations write to the Holiday Inn Crowne Plaza, 120 South Wildwood Drive, Branson, Missouri 65616, or call 1-800-428-3386.

Indian Pointe Resorts

Indian Pointe Resorts is actually three resorts: Indian Pointe Lodge, Trail's End Resort, and Eagle View Cottages.

You don't have to be a fisherman to enjoy any or all of these three resorts. Dyed-in-the-wool fishermen return here each year to have a go at the incredible fishing bounty of Table Rock Lake, but non-sportsmen and their families have also discovered that each of these fine resorts is an ideal place to stay while enjoying the music and shopping in Branson and the spectacular scenery of the Ozark Mountains.

Indian Pointe Lodge and Trail's End Resort are located right on the lake and are extremely accessible to the boat docks, fishing, and other water-related activities. The visitor has a number of choices when it comes to rooms, and the prices are quite competitive.

The Eagle View Cottages are located atop a wooded ridge and offer a breathtaking view of Table Rock Lake. The individual cottages are painted in pastel colors and feature gingerbread trim and Victorian decor. A quiet and pleasurable peacefulness and serenity reign here.

For more information write to Indian Pointe Resorts, HC 1, Box 982, Branson, Missouri 65616, or call 1-800-888-1891.

Indian Trails Resort

One-, two-, and three-bedroom lakefront cottages, all immaculately clean, all with kitchenettes, are located on the lake at Indian Point and are only minutes away from downtown Branson.

Honeymooners, fishermen, and folks who just like to get away for a few days find the Indian Trails Resort a perfect place to stay during their Branson visit. Features include a swimming pool, boat dock, and boat ramp.

For information and reservations write to the Indian Trails Resort, HCR 1, Box 999 SA, Branson, Missouri 65616, or call (417) 338-2327.

The Inn at Fall Creek

A Victorian ambience is associated with this fine bed and breakfast set in a wooded glade not far from Branson's finest show places and restaurants. The Inn at Fall Creek offers a great big deck accompanied by a great view. The three rooms and two suites are attractive, clean, and inviting. The breakfasts here are delicious and no one ever goes away hungry.

For information and reservations write to The Inn at Fall Creek, 391 Concord Avenue, Branson, Missouri 65616, or call 1-800-280-3422.

Journey's End Bed and Breakfast

Journey's End has two units: One is a hand-hewn log cabin and contains a fireplace, four-poster bed, and screened-in back porch; the other is a three-room frame building that can accommodate four people.

Unlike a lot of breakfasts at bed and breakfast places, this one is delivered to your room in the morning so you can eat out on the porch!

For information or reservations write Journey's End Bed and Breakfast, Missouri Highway 76 West, Branson, or call (417) 338-2685

Kimberling Inn

A lot of people who visit Branson like to find lodging a short distance away in order to get away from the hustle and bustle of traffic and crowds. More and more, the Kimberling Inn Resort is accommodating these folks. Located on Table Rock Lake, the Kimberling Inn Resort has three outdoor pools and one indoor pool, sauna, hot tub, steam room, health club, tennis courts, eighteen-hole miniature golf course, a boat ramp, and even lighted boat stalls. The

Kimberling Inn is a favored location for tour groups, weddings, conferences, and reunions.

For more information on the Kimberling Inn Resort and Conference Center, write P.O. Box 159, Kimberling City, Missouri 65686, or call 1-800-833-5551.

Lakeshore Resort

A charming getaway located on the lake in a nice, quiet, wooded area, the Lakeshore Resort can fill the bill for a number of needs: Fishermen love it, honeymooners love it, families love it, and any and all types of vacationers love it. Convenient to downtown Branson, the Lakeshore offers a pleasant deck, fireplaces in the rooms, and a playground for the kids.

For information or reservations write 1773 Lakeshore Drive, Branson, Missouri, 65616, or call 1-800-583-6101.

Leisure Country Inn

One of the handy features of the Leisure Country Inn is that these nice folks will prearrange your Branson vacation, offering customized packages with your choice of shows. In an instant, they can provide information about ticket prices and availability. The packages, including show tickets, rooms, continental breakfasts, and area discount coupons, range from $185 to $361, depending on how long you stay and the type of accommodations you prefer.

The Leisure Country Inn is a clean, tidy and well-run place operated by friendly and helpful people. The Inn features elevators, guest laundry, outdoor pool, hot tub, exercise room, and free local calls.

For more information write Leisure Country Inn, 3350 West Highway 76, Branson, Missouri 65616, or call 1-800-655-7330.

Lilley's Landing

The Lake Taneycomo location of Lilley's Landing makes it convenient not only to Branson visitors but to trout fishermen also. The lake is only a few steps from your room, boats and motors rental are available, and a guide service is even provided. The one- to four-bedroom cabins, all nicely appointed, have kitchenettes. There is a swimming pool, a playground, a horseshoe pitching court, and barbecue grills for cooking and picnicking outdoors.

For more information write HCR 5, Box 2170, Branson, Missouri 65616, or call 1-800-264-2483.

Lodge of the Ozarks

During our visit to the Lodge of the Ozarks, we learned that former Vice President Robert Dole and his wife, Elizabeth, stayed here in 1992. If their experience was similar to ours, they must have loved this place.

This entertainment complex offers nearly 200 large rooms, convenience to downtown, a theater, hair and nail salon, swimming pool, snack bar, and gift shop. The family that stays at the Lodge of the Ozarks is within short walking distance to literally dozens of showplaces, dining, and shopping.

Friendly, helpful staff see to it that you want for nothing. For more information or reservations write to Lodge of the Ozarks, 3431 76 Country Boulevard, Branson, Missouri 65616, or call (417) 334-7535.

Melody Lane Inn

We have been told that the fine folks who own this comfortable inn also own the Palace Inn. It proves they know something about how to take good care of a visitor.

The Melody Lane Inn boasts a glorious setting, overlooking a wooded area and just far enough away from the main road to be reasonably quiet. Here you can find 140 rooms and a nice, large, heated outdoor swimming pool.

For more information or reservations write to the Melody Lane Inn, 2821 76 Country Boulevard, Branson, Missouri 65616, or call 1-800-338-8598.

Old Matt's Guest House Motel

Like Aunt Mollie's Boarding House, Old Matt's Guest House Motel was named after one of the principal characters in Harold Bell Wright's great play *The Shepherd of the Hills*. This is no coincidence, for both establishments are owned by the same folks who own the Shepherd of the Hills Homestead.

Old Matt's rooms are reasonably priced and close to Branson's showplaces and restaurants. For more information write 3306 Shepherd of the Hills Expressway, or call (417) 334-0031.

Ozark Mountain Resort

Nestled comfortably in a mountainside location close to the shores of Table Rock Lake, Ozark Mountain Resort offers just about anything the traveler could want: Olympic-size outdoor pool, hot tub, exercise room, sauna, dressing room and showers, tennis court, covered boat dock, archery range, basketball court, volleyball, guide service, boat ramp, swimming beach, children's playground, horseback riding, miniature golf, and much more.

The friendly staff and reasonable prices make the Ozark Mountain Resort a popular location with Branson visitors.

For more information write Ozark Mountain Resort, HCR 4, Box 910, Kimberling City, Missouri 65686, or call 1-800-225-2422.

Palace Inn

Thousands and thousands of Branson visitors who have stayed at the Palace Inn perceive this fine establishment as the premier place to stay for a number of reasons. Great accommodations can be found here, and the visitor is within walking distance to a number of popular showplaces, great restaurants, and excellent shopping.

Spacious rooms, nice appointments, handsome furniture, and other features provide for a comfortable stay at the Palace Inn. A wide selection of rooms and beds are available, as are suites. There is even a penthouse if you really want to impress someone.

For more information or reservations write to the Palace Inn, 2820 76 Country Boulevard, Branson, Missouri 65616, or call 1-800-725-2236.

Plantation Inn

Like many fine Branson inns, the Plantation is conveniently located close to the heart of the town's action. Many of the people who stay here are repeat visitors. Moms love the shopping at the nearby mall, the kids love, in addition to the inn's swimming pool, the many diversions available to them up and down the strip, and dads love all of the excellent restaurants, including the one located at the inn. Practically anytime during the day, the entire family can leave from the Plantation and, within minutes, attend any one of several great live performances.

Very reasonably priced, the Plantation Inn also offers a nice selection of dinner and show packages. For more information write 3470 Keeter Street, Branson, Missouri 65616, or call (417) 334-3600.

Pointe Royale

The Pointe Royale Condominium is a luxury home away from home. One-, two-, and three-bedroom condos are available for families, groups, reunions, and any kind of special gathering. Each condo has a fully equipped kitchen and a private patio or deck that looks out over the fascinating Ozark scenery. There exists numerous opportunities for privacy or for mingling with kindred spirits.

Only minutes away from the shows, the lake, and shopping, this resort boasts an eighteen-hole championship golf course, one of the most popular in the area.

The Pointe Royale features, in addition to the fine golf course, a magnificent swimming pool, a lakeside trout-fishing park, as well as swimming, skiing, fishing, boating, and marina services.

For information write Pointe Royale, 158-A Pointe Royale Drive, Branson, Missouri 65616, or call 1-800-962-4710.

Queen Anne I

Convenience is one of the principal attractions of the Queen Anne I. Located right on the entertainment strip, this comfortable forty-room motel has a heated outdoor pool, plenty of parking, and a continental breakfast.

For more information write 3510 76 Country Boulevard, or call (417) 335-8100.

Queen Anne II

The Queen Anne II is similar to the Queen Anne I but is located a bit farther away from the traffic and crowds. Eighty-eight rooms are pleasantly nestled in a wooded area. There is also a heated swimming pool and a continental breakfast. If you stay at the Queen Anne II, you are invited to drive to the Queen Anne I and leave your vehicle on their parking lot as you walk to the many fine shows, shopping areas, and restaurants on the strip.

For information or reservations write 245 Schaefer Drive, or call (417) 335-8101.

Ramada

Actually called the Branson Grand Ramada, this new, huge hotel has it all—convenient location, grand furnishings, a fine continental breakfast, indoor pool, hot tub, sauna, exercise room, hair salon, and gift shop. A number of different kinds of rooms are available, and the prices are quite competitive and affordable.

For information or reservations write to the Branson Grand Ramada, 245 North Wildwood Drive, Branson, Missouri 65616, or call (417) 336-6646.

Rhapsody Bed and Breakfast Inn

A pleasant Victorian feel greets the visitor to the Rhapsody, a delightful, comfortable, and very reasonably priced bed and breakfast. The Rhapsody has twelve rooms, some of which have Jacuzzis, and one of which is accessible to the handicapped. If you want a great view, great accommodations, and a great breakfast, the Rhapsody is the place for you.

For information or reservations write to 296 Blue Meadows Road, Branson, or call 1-800-790-3892.

River Pointe Estates

Located just a few short miles from Branson near the College of the Ozarks, the River Pointe Estates offer, as their advertising says, "Trout Fishing At Its Best Surrounded By Serenity And Luxury." In this case, it's all true.

One-, two-, and three-bedroom condominiums are attractively nestled into an environment consisting of grassy sward and woodland. Everything the fisherman needs is here: covered boat docks, boat rentals, and, of course, great fishing. The rest of the family will enjoy the large pool, tennis courts, horseshoe pitching, and children's playground. In addition, one also finds fireplaces, guest laundry, and banquet and conference facilities.

For more information or reservations write P.O. Box 966, Branson, Missouri 65616, or call 1-800-633-5358.

Rockwood Resort

"Vacations are friendlier at Rockwood Resort," says the advertising, and guests will tell you that is certainly true. Located on Table Rock Lake only ten minutes away from shows, shopping, and dining, the Rockwood is a treat for fishermen and families. The prices here are surprisingly reasonable for these clean, fully equipped rooms. Cable television, swimming pool, and picnic area appeal to the kids while dad is catching fish. Boat and motor rentals are available, and the covered and lighted boat dock, as well as a boat ramp, remain busy.

For information or reservations write Rockwood Resort, SR 1, Box 1162, Branson, Missouri 65616, or call 1-800-276-6667.

Sammy Lane Resort

The Sammy Lane Resort, like a few other places in Branson, is named after a character in Harold Bell Wright's *The Shepherd of the Hills*. The Sammy Lane has been around and serving fishermen and other Branson visitors for over seventy years, so it's got to have a lot of positive elements going for it. One is convenience. Located right on the shore of Lake Taneycomo, this great place is a two-minute walk from old downtown Branson and within short driving distance to all of the shows, shopping, and restaurants.

You've got to see the Sammy Lane to believe it. It has a huge swimming pool, probably the largest one in the area, and the cabins are on the National Register of Historic Places.

There is nice selection of accommodations here: One- and two-bedroom units are available, some units have kitchenettes, and all have cable television.

Get your reservations early if you want to stay here. For more information write 320 East Main Street, or call (417) 334-3253.

Settle Inn

The Settle Inn is not your typical motel. If you want something different, try this one on for size.

For starters, the Settle Inn has everything you want in a fine luxury motel, including two indoor swimming pools, whirlpools, tanning booths, and a gift shop. The dark wood furniture that graces each of the rooms is handsome and well cared for.

So what's so different about this place? On Wednesday and Fridays, an audience-participation Murder Mystery Dinner Theater is performed. This is all-out pure fun, and if you happen to interpret the clues and determine the identity of the murderer, you can win a prize!

There's more. The Settle Inn has theme rooms that are almost as much fun as the dinner theater. Try the Saturday Night Fever Disco Room, the Bedrock Room, or the Observatory Room for something a little different. You won't be disappointed.

In addition, the Settle Inn provides a hot breakfast accompanied by an entertaining morning show.

For information or reservations write 3050 Green Mountain Drive, Branson, Missouri 65616, or call 1-800-677-6906.

The 76 Mall Inn

The 76-business complex includes not only this fine inn, but a great music hall featuring several shows daily, a quality restaurant, indoor miniature golf, an arcade, and over 35,000 square feet of shopping. A vast parking lot can accommodate not only cars and pickups, but also large motor homes and recreational vehicles.

The 76 Mall Inn contains over 300 rather spacious rooms. Cable television is standard. The two swimming pools (indoor and outdoor) tempt many visitors. Morning coffee is waiting for you in the office.

For information and reservations as well as special vacation packages, write to 1945 76 Country Boulevard, Branson, Missouri 65616, or call (417) 335-3535.

ShadowBrook Motel

Sixty rooms, each of which overlooks a wooded area, is one of the many things that attract people to the Shadow-Brook. Located on twenty-seven acres of grassy sward and woodland, the ShadowBrook offers clean, surprisingly inexpensive, and rather cozy rooms. A friendly and efficient staff provide for a pleasant stay. The free continental breakfast is a great place and time for visitors to get together and visit. New friends are made here every day.

For more information or reservations write to the ShadowBrook Motel, 1610 76 Country Boulevard, Branson, Missouri 65616, or call (417) 334-4173.

Silver Fountain Inn

Located in the heart of the Branson action, the Silver Fountain Inn has been around for a least a couple of decades and is still accommodating visitors to these Ozark hills in fine fashion.

Rooms at the Silver Fountain Inn look out over a pleasant, shady valley, yet this nice complex is almost in the shade of Dolly Parton's Dixie Stampede.

Reasonably priced, the Silver Fountain Inn features a nice swimming pool, as well as a tiny pool for babies, and a free continental breakfast.

For more information or reservations write to 1425 76 Country Boulevard, or call (417) 334-5125.

Southern Oaks Inn

This comfortable and friendly 150-room inn is located close to the ever-popular IMAX Theater and Shoji Tabuchi's showplace. Two swimming pools (indoor and outdoor) are busy during the summer. Other features include a hot tub, continental breakfast, and a large parking lot to accommodate all kinds of vehicles.

For more information or reservations write 3295 Shepherd of the Hills Expressway, or call 1-800-324-8752.

Still Waters Condominium Resort

Located two miles south of Silver Dollar City and only minutes from shopping, dining, and the Branson entertainment center, Still Waters offers a bit of everything for the entire family. Boaters and fishermen love this resort, and access to the lake can be undertaken from three different boat docks. Resort features include three swimming pools, tennis courts, volleyball courts, playgrounds, jet ski rentals, paddleboats (free!), poolside hot tubs, laundry, and more.

A variety of accommodations are available ranging from one-, two-, and three-bedroom suites with Jacuzzis to deluxe hotel rooms. Vacation packages begin at $169.

For more information about Still Waters write HC1, Box 928, Branson, Missouri 65616, or call 1-800-777-2320.

Stonewall Motor Inn

This clean, quiet little inn is located in the colorful older section of downtown Branson and is within walking distance of Lake Taneycomo and a number of fine eateries. A short drive will bring the visitor directly to the heart of the entertainment and shopping district.

Rates are extremely reasonable at the Stonewall Motor Inn. Write for reservations at 511 South Commercial Street, Branson, Missouri, or call (417) 334-3416.

Stonewall West

The Stonewall West is owned and operated by the same folks who run the Stonewall Motor Inn (see above). As a result, the same friendly service and clean, reasonably priced accommodations are available. The Stonewall West also has a swimming pool.

Considered one of the best deals in Branson, Stonewall West is conveniently located at the intersection of 76 Country Boulevard and Roark Valley Road and is ideally situated for those who wish to shop, dine, attend musical performances, and even fish on Table Rock Lake or Lake Taneycomo.

For more information write 1040 76 Country Boulevard, Branson, Missouri 65616, or call (417) 334-5173.

Thousand Hills Golf Resort

If you are looking for a luxury golf resort, Thousand Hills is the place for you. Along with all of the other amenities, an eighteen-hole championship golf course beckons. On the other hand, you don't have to be a golfer to love this place. Featuring 170 new one-, two-, and three-bedroom condominiums and hotel rooms, Thousand Oaks also offers swimming pools, whirlpool tubs, fully equipped kitchens, tennis courts, and conference facilities.

For more information or reservations write 245 South Wildwood Drive, Branson, Missouri 65616, or call 1-800-864-4145.

Treehouse on the Lake

Located right on beautiful Table Rock Lake, Treehouse has been designed such that every condo has a great view. Quiet, peaceful, and serene, Treehouse is only minutes away from downtown Branson.

To receive an information packet write HCR 1, Box 1163-12, Branson, Missouri 65616, or call (417) 338-5199.

Trout Hollow Lodge

If you want to be close to downtown Branson, yet prefer to relax and sleep in the quiet and peaceful comfort of the country, then the Trout Hollow Lodge is the place for you.

If you are a fisherman, the Trout Hollow Lodge has everything you would ever want: a full service marina, 260-foot-long fishing dock, lighted and covered boat slips, boat rental, and bait and tackle shop. There is even a guide service available here.

One-, two-, and three-bedroom cabins with kitchenettes await the weary traveler. The lodge also features a large swimming pool and color television.

For reservations or more information write 1458 Acacia Club Road, Branson, Missouri 65616, or call 1-800-328-1246.

Turkey Creek Ranch

Called "the lake resort with a dude ranch flavor," this great place offers a little something different for visitors.

This is an actual 400-acre working ranch located in the wooded Ozarks close to the lake, complete with cows and horses. Here you can find some great horseback riding, two swimming pools (indoor and outdoor), tennis courts, boat docks, and all kinds of boats (bass boats, sailboats, pontoon boats, canoes, and paddleboats). There is a recreation room containing pool tables, a game room, and shuffleboard. There is also a fine restaurant on the premises.

Seventeen cottages are available, all fully equipped. They are set in a quiet and peaceful environment on Bull Shoals Lake about twenty-five miles east of Branson, sufficiently away from the traffic and crowds.

For information or reservations write to the Turkey Creek Ranch, HC 3, Box 3180-S93, Theodosia, Missouri 65761

Twin Island Resort

Just a few miles south of and fifteen minutes away from Branson and on the shores of beautiful Table Rock Lake can be found the Twin Island Resort. More and more travelers are discovering this pleasant and comfortable resort, much to their delight and enjoyment.

The Twin Island may be one of the best places to fish on the lake. At the Twin Island, the fisherman finds everything he needs plus more: covered and lighted boat dock with electrical outlets, fish cleaning station, freezer storage for your catch, bait and tackle, boat rental, and a free guide service. Special fisherman vacation packages are available.

In spite of all of the attention given to the fishermen, families are not neglected in the least. At the Twin Island Resort, one and all can enjoy the swimming pool, tubing, water skiing, and the gorgeous picnic area with grills and tables.

For information or reservations write to Twin Island Resort, 4134 State Highway 86, Ridgedale, Missouri 65739, or call 1-800-499-2986.

Welk Resort Hotel

The Welk Resort Hotel is part of the giant Lawrence Welk complex, which includes the theater and restaurant. This four-story hotel contains 158 very nice rooms, several of which are designed for the handicapped and hearing impaired. Kids are provided with hand-held video games for their entertainment. The hotel also offers a heated swimming pool, horseshoes, a croquet court, and one of the best continental breakfasts in town.

Several different vacation packages can be obtained from the friendly staff. For information and reservations write 1984, Missouri Highway 165, or call 1-800-505-WELK.

The Woods Resort

As the name implies, The Woods Resort offers 180 motel rooms and 25 log cabins (fully equipped) nestled in a quiet wooded area, yet it is close to the Shepherd of the Hills Expressway.

The Woods offers a nice-sized outdoor swimming pool, continental breakfast, pleasant and scenic hiking trails, shuffleboard court, and volleyball court.

For more information write 2201 Roark Valley Road, or call 1-800-935-2345.

Section Sixteen

Festivals

Throughout the year, a number of annual fairs, festivals, and conventions are held in and around Branson. Some have said there are more fairs and festivals in the Ozarks each year than in any other part of the country. Themes range from fiddlers' gatherings to art shows to fishing competitions. Great bargains and entertainment are normally found at many of these fairs, and visitors arrive from all fifty of the United States as well as several foreign countries in order to participate in the gatherings.

Many of these annual and seasonal festivals have been going on for generations, others are relatively new, and more are being added every year.

Some of the more popular and well-known festivals include the following:

Artsfest

The Artsfest is held in May of each year in Springfield, Missouri, about forty miles north of Branson. This festival lasts for two days and provides an opportunity for dozens of local artists and craftsmen to display and sell their products. Entertainment, lots of food, and a number of activities accompany the arts and crafts show for children. And the admission is only a buck. Kids under twelve are free! You can't beat it.

For specific times and information call (417) 869-8380.

Autumn Days Craft Festival

Branson may be the home for more craft festivals than any other city in the United States. This one, which takes place during the month of September, features over 100 artists and craftsmen who display their products and sell them at great bargain prices. As with any good craft show, this one is replete with lots of good food and entertainment.

Blues Festival

The Eureka Springs Blues Festival is a well-attended series of events that take place over the course of a week during the month of June. Top blues and jazz performers perform in concert all week long, and the local clubs and cabarets are filled with blues fans who come to listen to the local and regional artists play.

For more information call (501) 253-5366.

Branson Fan Fest

Not only is this a fan fest, it is a *fun* fest! Many of Branson's favorite entertainers gather to perform and sign autographs. Here is your chance to shake hands and rub shoulders with some of the country's most prominent entertainers, hear some great music, and partake of some of the wonderful food brought in by area restaurants. And one of the best parts of this annual festival is that all profits are donated to area charities.

Branson Fan Fest occurs in March every year. For more information call (417) 334-4136.

Fall Festival

Held each year in October at Rockaway Beach on the shore of Lake Taneycomo, this exciting event features all kinds of entertainment, crafts, and some fine dining. For information on specific times call (417) 561-4280.

Festival of Lights

During the months of November and December, Branson sparkles like a giant diamond from all of the special lights. The best way to see this stunning display is from an airplane, but lacking one, simply drive through town, shopping centers, and the area neighborhoods to enjoy and marvel at the glowing and colorful displays.

Fiddlers Convention

The State of the Ozarks Fiddlers Convention is now held every year at Branson's Compton Ridge Campground (see Section Nine, Outdoor Recreation). If you like fiddle music or if you play fiddle music, this is *the* place to be. Fiddlers perform in concert, and many just jam with one another on the grounds from dawn to way past dusk. All kinds of fiddlin' competition is conducted, and the hills simply ring with music for days.

The State of the Ozarks Fiddlers Convention takes place twice each year, May and September. For information on times and location call (417) 338-2911.

Fine Arts Festival

The Fine Arts Festival takes place in May of each year in scenic, historic, and always entertaining Eureka Springs, Arkansas, about a one-hour drive from Branson.

Forsyth Art Guild Annual Craft Show

Each year, the members of the Forsyth Art Guild sponsor the Annual Craft Show. Area artists display and sell their wares. Some truly fine water colors, oils, acrylics, and other media can be found at this enjoyable gathering. In addition, local craftsmen display and sell everything from furniture to musical instruments to dolls.

The Forsyth Art Guild Annual Craft Show takes place in March every year. For specific times call (417) 546-5439.

Forsyth Art Guild Spring China Show

The Forsyth Art Guild is an active bunch of nice folks who put on some grand shows. The Spring China Show is an excellent place for area porcelain and china painters to display their work. Many beautiful pieces and great bargains on decorative objects can be found.

The Forsyth Art Guild Spring China Show takes place in April. For more information on specific times call (417) 546-5439.

Free Fall Harvest Festival

Held on the grounds of the Shepherd of the Hills theme park, the Free Fall Harvest Festival is one of the best arts and crafts events in the region. Lots of booths, lots of great bargains, and lots of tasty food greet the visitor to this assemblage of some of the region's finest artists and craftsmen.

The Free Fall Harvest Festival takes place during September. For information on specific times call (417) 334-4191.

The Great American Music Festival

Silver Dollar City is the location for the Great American Music Festival, an event that brings musicians from throughout the country to participate in this fun-filled gathering. Formal concerts are produced, but a lot of spontaneous jam sessions under the shade trees take place.

The Great American Music Festival takes place during the month of June. For information on specific times call 1-800-952-6626.

Harvest Moon Fall Festival

Branson neighbor Forsyth is the setting for the Harvest Moon Fall Festival. There is lots of fun to be had here for kids and adults alike, including music, crafts, and food. It takes place at Shadow Rock Park, everyone is invited, and there is no admission charge.

The Harvest Moon Fall Festival takes place during September. For information on specific times call (417) 546-2741.

Kewpiesta

The name of this annual gathering is derived from "kewpie doll." Indeed, collecting kewpie dolls has become a national craze in recent years, and some of the country's most avid collectors and experts on kewpie dolls come to the southwestern Missouri Ozarks each year to display, share, trade, and discuss kewpiana.

The kewpie doll, incidentally, was first designed by Ozark native Rosie O'Neill in 1908. She was from this area.

Kewpiesta takes place each April. For more information on time and place call 1-800-539-7437.

May Fine Arts Festival

The month of May in Eureka Springs is one of the most exciting times of the year for that exciting town. The fine arts festival, which lasts the entire month, includes special music and concerts, art shows and exhibitions, and food, food, food!

For more information call (501) 253-8737.

National Children's Festival

The National Children's Festival is yet one more thing that Silver Dollar City does well. Billed as the largest children's festival in the world, it features well over 100 activities and events for youngsters. Silver Dollar City has teamed up with the television network Nickelodeon to provide much of the fun.

The National Children's Festival takes place during June. For information on specific times call 1-800-952-6626.

National Festival of Craftsmen

This is the creme de la creme of craft shows. Held on the grounds of the Silver Dollar City theme park, this stunning event features potters, woodcarvers, artists, stained glass craftsmen, broom-makers, basket weavers, and more. You get to watch them fashion their stunning creations up close and personal, and they will answer your questions. Complete with displays, booths, and some great food, this is a festival you don't want to miss.

The National Festival of Craftsmen is held during parts of September and October. For specific information on times call 1-800-952-6626.

Ozark Mountain Christmas

You have never celebrated Christmas like this before. Holiday spirit and revelry is something altogether different in the Ozarks, and it is something you will return to experience year after year. Craft shows, fairs, parades, sales, and numerous special events fill the schedule and keep you hopping from one end of town to the other.

For specific times, call (417) 334-4136.

Passion Play

The town of Eureka Springs, Arkansas, located about thirty-five miles southwest of Branson, is host each year to The Great Passion Play. This well-acted and professionally produced performance chronicles the life of Jesus through his crucifixion, burial, and ascension.

Each year, The Great Passion Play performs to rave reviews. Sets and costumes are unmatched anywhere. The play is performed Monday through Thursday April through October. Thousands attend this fine performance, many coming from Europe and Canada.

Reservations are required for The Great Passion Play. For more information call 1-800-882-7529.

Plumb Nellie Days

A more appropriate name for this event might be "Ozark Hillbilly Days." An arts and crafts show is scheduled, along with a parade, and the crowning of the Plumb Nellie Days King and Queen. Local merchants and citizens deck out in their hillbilly finest—overalls, corncob pipes, slouch hats, and all the rest. There is also a beard-growing contest and, get this, an outhouse race!

Plumb Nellie Days take place in May. For information on specific times call (417) 334-1458.

Taney County Fair

If you like county fairs, the Taney County version, held at the county seat of Forsyth, is well worth a visit. Conducted in July of each year, this fun-filled fair features everything from foods to rides to games to arts and crafts. Forsyth is just a few minutes' drive from Branson.

For more information call (417) 546-2741.

Veterans' Homecoming

Each year, thousands of veterans arrive at Branson to participate in A Veteran's Homecoming. Parades, celebrations, and special shows and programs at many of the town's theaters and music halls honor military veterans and their contributions to the United States. There is nothing like this celebration anywhere, and you don't have to be a veteran to appreciate it.

A Veterans' Homecoming takes place during November. For information on specific times call (417) 334-4136.

War Eagle Antique and Crafts Show

The War Eagle Show is one of the largest in this part of the United States, is growing every year, and has become *the* place for artists, craftsmen, authors, potters, weavers, quilters, dollmakers, and others to display and sell their wares. Travelers arrive from thousands of miles away each year to participate in this grand show.

The setting is gorgeous—a real, operational water-powered mill is on the premises, and the alternately woody and grassy environments are pleasant.

In addition to the incredibly large and eclectic collection of antiques, crafts, and art, the food available at this gathering is among the finest you will find at a crafts fair anywhere, bar none. Practically everything can be found here, from roast beef to snow cones.

The War Eagle Mill Spring Antique and Crafts Show occurs twice each year in War Eagle, Arkansas (about fifty miles southwest of Branson), once in May and once in October. For information call (501) 789-5343 or (501) 789-5398.

The White Bass Round-Up

If bass fishing is your forte, you will enjoy this tournament. For most of March and through the first half of May, fisherman flock to Bull Shoals Lake for this nine-week competition. Cash prizes are given in several categories, and the event is culminated with a big fish fry.

Headquarters for The White Bass Round-Up are in nearby Forsyth. For more information call (417) 546-2741.

Wood Carving Rendezvous

The Annual Woodcarving Rendezvous is held at Compton Ridge Campground during the month of June. A week of seminars oriented toward beginners as well as advanced and professional carvers is well attended, drawing artists from around the country.

For information on specific times call (913) 631-0306.

World Fest

Silver Dollar City is the site for this assemblage of world-class performers. A global theme is apparent here, as many of the entertainers arrive from foreign countries for this fun-filled festival. Jugglers, musicians, dancers, clowns, and magicians are just a few of the attractions at World Fest.

Accompanying the shows and acts is a wide variety of cuisines representative of several different nations.

World Fest is a huge gathering, attracting thousands from around the country each year. The events commence around the last week of April and continue through early May.

For information on specific times and admission costs call 1-800-952-6626.

Section Seventeen

Branson Trivia: Some Interesting and Little Known Facts

Did you know that . . .

1. The mega-production "Branson City Lights" at the Remington Theater cost nearly $8 million dollars to produce. This cost includes the over 150,000 rhinestones sewn onto the costumes as well as $85,000 worth of feathers!

2. Ronnie Milsap, a popular Branson performer, has been inducted into two different state music halls of fame: Georgia and North Carolina.

3. Speaking of Ronnie Milsap, he performed for two years at his own theater in Myrtle Beach, South Carolina, before coming to Branson.

4. The Golden Girls, who perform regularly at the Country Tonight Theater, are all fifty years of age or older!

5. Tony Orlando began his musical career in New York City writing songs on Tin Pan Alley with the likes of recording stars Neil Sedaka and Carole King.

6. Yakov Smirnov, Branson's popular comedian, was sworn in as an American citizen in 1986 at the Statue of Liberty!

7. Branson performer Wayne Newton appeared as the featured entertainer at the Ronald Reagan White House before a crowd of 390,000 people!

8. The biggest Veterans' Day celebration in the United States is held in Branson each year with more than fifty special events featured.

9. William Golding, one of the Oak Ridge Boys, lives in a real Indian teepee when he is home in Louisiana.

10. The Inspiration Tower, located at the Shepherd of the Hills Theme Park, contains over 92,000 pounds of structural steel, weighs just over 3,000,000 pounds, and is 230 ft., 10 inches tall.

11. Inspiration Tower contains over 4,400 square feet of glass—enough to cover one-third of a football field.

12. If you dropped an object from the open air observation deck of Inspiration Tower, it would strike the ground in 2.98 seconds at a speed of sixty-five miles per hour!

References

Castleman, Harvey N. *The Bald Knobbers, Story of the Lawless Nightriders Who Raided Southern Missouri in the 80s*. Girard, Kansas: Haldeman-Julius Publications. 1944.

Dougan, Michael B. *Arkansas Odyssey: The Saga of Arkansas from Prehistoric Times to the Present*. Little Rock: Rose Publishing Co., Inc. 1994.

Hartman, Mary, and Ingenthron, Elmo. *Bald Knobbers: Vigilantes on the Ozarks Frontier*. Gretna, Louisiana: Pelican Publishing Company. 1988.

Jameson, W.C. *Buried Treasures of the Ozarks*. Little Rock, Arkansas: August House, Inc. 1990.

Keefe, James F., and Morrow, Lynn. *The White River Chronicles of S.C. Turnbo: Man and Wildlife on the Ozarks Frontier*. Fayetteville, Arkansas: University of Arkansas Press.

Rafferty, Milton D. *The Ozarks Outdoors: A Guide For Fishermen, Hunters, and Tourists*. Norman: University of Oklahoma Press. 1985.

Wright, Steve. *Ozark Trout Tales*. Fayetteville, Arkansas: White River Chronicle. 1995.

Index

Republic of Texas Press

100 Days in Texas: The Alamo
Letters
by Wallace O. Chariton

Alamo Movies
by Frank Thompson

**At Least 1836 Things You Ought
to Know About Texas but
Probably Don't**
by Doris L. Miller

Battlefields of Texas
by Bill Groneman

Best Tales of Texas Ghosts
by Docia Schultz Williams

**Bubba Speak: A Texas
Dictionary**
by W.C. Jameson

**Civil War Recollections of James
Lemuel Clark and the Great
Hanging at Gainesville, Texas in
October 1862**
by L.D. Clark

**Cow Pasture Pool: Golf on the
Muni-tour**
by Joe E. Winter

A Cowboy of Pecos
by Patrick Dearen

Cripple Creek Bonanza
by Chet Cunningham

**Daughter of Fortune: The Bettie
Brown Story**
by Sherrie S. McLeRoy

**Defense of a Legend: Crockett
and the de la Peña Diary**
by Bill Groneman

**Don't Throw Feathers at
Chickens: A Collection of Texas
Political Humor**
by Charles Herring, Jr. and Walter
Richter

**Eight Bright Candles:
Courageous Women of Mexico**
by Doris E. Perlin

**Etta Place: Her Life and Times
with Butch Cassidy and the
Sundance Kid**
by Gail Drago

**Exiled: The Tigua Indians of
Ysleta del Sur**
by Randy Lee Eickhoff

**Exploring Dallas with Children:
A Guide for Family Activities
(2nd Ed.)**
by Kay McCasland Threadgill

**Exploring San Antonio with
Children: A Guide for Family
Activities**
by Docia Schultz Williams

Exploring the Alamo Legends
by Wallace O. Chariton

Eyewitness to the Alamo
by Bill Groneman

First in the Lone Star State
by Sherrie S. McLeRoy

The Funny Side of Texas
by Ellis Posey and John Johnson

Ghosts Along the Texas Coast
by Docia Schultz Williams

The Great Texas Airship Mystery
by Wallace O. Chariton

**Henry Ossian Flipper, West
Point's First Black Graduate**
by Jane Eppinga

**Horses and Horse Sense: The
Practical Science of Horse
Husbandry**
by James "Doc" Blakely

**How the Cimarron River Got Its
Name and Other Stories About
Coffee**
by Ernestine Sewell Linck

The Last Great Days of Radio
by Lynn Woolley

**Last of the Old-Time Cowboys,
The**
by Patrick Dearen

Call Wordware Publishing, Inc. for names of the bookstores in your area
(972) 423-0090

Republic of Texas Press (Cont.)

Call Wordware Publishing, Inc. for names of the bookstores in your area
(972) 423-0090

Seaside Press

Critter Chronicles
by Jim Dunlap

Dallas Uncovered (2nd Edition)
by Larenda Lyles Roberts and Kay
Threadgill

**Dirty Dining: A Cookbook, and
More, for Lovers**
by Ginnie Siena Bivona

**Exotic Pets: A Veterinary Guide
for Owners**
by Shawn Messonnier, D.V.M.

Exploring Branson
by W.C. Jameson

**I Never Wanted to Set the World
on Fire, but Now That I'm 50,
Maybe It's a Good Idea**
by Bob Basso, Ph.D.

Jackson Hole Uncovered
by Sierra Sterling Adare

Just Passing Through
by Beth Beggs

Los Angeles Uncovered
by Frank Thompson

New Orleans Uncovered
by Larenda Lyles Roberts

Only: The Last Dinosaur
by Jim Dunlap

**Pete the Python: The Further
Adventures of Mark and Deke**
by Jim Dunlap

Salt Lake City Uncovered
by Sierra Adare and Candy Moulton

San Antonio Uncovered
by Mark Louis Rybczyk

San Francisco Uncovered
by Larenda Lyles Roberts

Seattle Uncovered
by JoAnn Roe

**They Don't Have to Die (2nd
Ed.)**
by Jim Dunlap

Tucson Uncovered
by John and Donna Kamper

Twin Cities Uncovered
by The Arthurs

Vancouver Uncovered
by JoAnn Roe

Your Puppy's First Year
by Shawn Messonnier, D.V.M.

Your Kitten's First Year
by Shawn Messonnier, D.V.M.

Call Wordware Publishing, Inc. for names of the bookstores in your area
(972) 423-0090